"Curt is adept at identifying and applying Scripture in winsome and practical ways to the many types of tensions and conflicts that plague human relationships, especially in the church. Most importantly, Curt loves the gospel of Christ and realizes that it provides the motive, the method, and the power for peacemaking."

from the foreword by **Ken Sande**, founder of Peacemaker Ministries and Relational Wisdom 360

"*The Peacemaking Church* provides exactly what Christians need to stop fighting *one another* and instead turn their attention toward fighting to protect the peace and purity of the church. If you are exhausted from the devastation of church conflict, you will be refreshed. If you are discouraged, you will find hope."

Tara Barthel, coauthor of *Redeeming Church Conflicts*, *Peacemaking Women*, and *Living the Gospel in Relationships*

"Don't miss this beautifully woven, transparent, amazing, and providential journey of grace! You and your church will be better prepared for the uncertain future we all face in a world and culture that seeks anything but unity."

David V. Edling, coauthor of *Redeeming Church Conflicts*

"Out of the pain of church conflict comes a refreshingly biblical and practical guide for building peace, resolving conflict, and preserving unity in the body of Christ. Get this book!"

Rev. Dr. Alfred Poirier, author of *The Peacemaking Pastor*

"Now here's a topic too often overlooked but never taken for granted by healthy churches. The honesty and biblical wisdom shared by Curtis Heffelfinger will do great good in any church willing to walk this path of grace and peace."

Collin Hansen, editorial director of the Gospel Coalition and author of *Blind Spots*

"Curtis Heffelfinger offers biblical help and counsel here. Pastors and church leaders will be instructed and edified as they think through his exposition and reflect on its application in their own local churches."

Ligon Duncan, PhD, chancellor and CEO of Reformed Theological Seminary

"I am grateful for Curt's timely and winsome book. Churches that lack a vision for peacemaking will find this book inspirational. Peacemakers seeking practical help on how to lead churches through conflict will find it rich with wisdom and guidance. I highly recommend church leaders read this gem and get a copy into the hands of their ministry team members as soon as possible."

Judy Dabler, president of Creative Conciliation

"Pastor Curt casts a vision for every church to become a true peacemaking church. This book is a refreshing personal testimony about how to resolve conflict in a biblically faithful manner and love others as Jesus loves us. I didn't want to put it down!"

Judy Steidl, COO of ICC Peace

"Curt delivers a cornucopia of rich peacemaking produce cultivated over decades of life as a son, husband, dad, and pastor. Pastors, church leaders, church members, and believers of all stripes will benefit from reading it. Putting its eight biblical keys into practice will inevitably lead to a harvest of peace. This book, as with Curt's life, has taught me much. It prompted a very healthy self-examination, one we all need regularly if we want to be agents of peace and unity within the relational matrices of our lives."

David A. Sims, JD, PhD, author of *The Child in American Evangelicalism* and *The Problem of Affluence*

"Curt humbly springs from his own pastoring experience to call all of us to, as Paul instructs, 'maintain the unity of the Spirit in the bond of peace.' We are to live—and walk and worship—together in love, humility, gentleness, and patience. With vivid storytelling, Curt demonstrates how making these choices in all our relationships and in our churches can bring us together in healing, respect, and kindness. And thus reflect to our broken world a true image of our Savior."

Judy Douglass, director of Women's Resources, Cru

THE
PEACE-
MAKING
CHURCH

8 Biblical Keys to Resolve Conflict
and Preserve Unity

CURTIS HEFFELFINGER

BakerBooks

a division of Baker Publishing Group
Grand Rapids, Michigan

© 2018 by Curtis Heffelfinger

Published by Baker Books
a division of Baker Publishing Group
PO Box 6287, Grand Rapids, MI 49516-6287
www.bakerbooks.com

Printed in the United States of America

Library of Congress Cataloging-in-Publication Data
Names: Heffelfinger, Curtis, 1952– author.
Title: The peacemaking church : 8 biblical keys to resolve conflict and preserve unity / Curtis
    Heffelfinger.
Description: Grand Rapids, MI : Baker Books, [2018] | Includes bibliographical references.
Identifiers: LCCN 2018008439 | ISBN 9780801019500 (pbk.)
Subjects: LCSH: Church controversies.
Classification: LCC BV652.9 .H435 2018 | DDC 253—dc23
LC record available at https://lccn.loc.gov/2018008439

Some names and details have been changed to protect the privacy of the individuals involved.

18 19 20 21 22 23 24   7 6 5 4 3 2 1

This book is dedicated to the covenant members
of Orlando Grace Church.
Thank you for being eager to preserve
the unity of the Spirit in the bond of peace.

Contents

Foreword

Where two or three come together in Jesus's name . . . there will soon be conflict.

This fact is reflected throughout the New Testament epistles, most of which deal with some kind of conflict in the early church.

These same types of conflict have kept me busy for thirty-five years.

As a full-time peacemaker and mediator, I have been involved in thousands of conflicts involving Christians. Divorces, child custody disputes, lawsuits between Christians, forced pastoral exits, church splits, abuse of children, even fistfights on the church board . . . you name it, I've seen it.

But I've also seen something else: the redeeming power of the gospel of Christ.

In case after case, when nearly everyone had given up hope of reconciliation, God suddenly broke through. Hearts softened. People finally saw and grieved over their sins. Confession replaced confrontation. Forgiveness replaced fighting.

Some of these breakthroughs were so dramatic they moved seasoned attorneys to tears. One lawyer was so caught up in the spirit of reconciliation that he pulled out his personal checkbook and asked to pay part of the damages his client finally admitted he owed to the opposing party. In another case, an attorney pulled me aside and said, "There is a power in this room. I can feel it. What is it?"

I love those questions . . . the answer, of course, is "Jesus Christ, the Prince of Peace!"

As wonderful as it is to see conflicts resolved and relationships restored, it is even better to see them prevented in the first place as people cultivate and practice the relational skills described in Scripture. This is why I love this book: it provides practical wisdom on how to resolve conflicts in the church, but even more importantly it shows how an entire congregation can cultivate character qualities and relational skills that will prevent most conflicts from starting in the first place.

I've known the author, Curt, for many years and have seen him grow as a peacemaker. Like me, Curt has made mistakes along the way . . . but he's learned from them, and he's passed those lessons on to the members of his church and to other pastors who have been inspired and instructed by his example. In this book, he is passing them on to you.

Better yet, Curt is a student of God's Word. As you'll see throughout this book, he is adept at identifying and applying Scripture in winsome and practical ways to the many types of tensions and conflicts that plague human relationships, especially in the church.

Most importantly, Curt loves the gospel of Christ and realizes that it provides the motive, the method, and the power for peacemaking. So in addition to describing a variety of wisdom principles and peacemaking skills, he consistently calls us to be inspired, guided, and empowered by Jesus and his example of sacrifice, redemption, forgiveness, and reconciliation.

So I encourage you, read on! Chapter by chapter, you will gain insights, feel conviction, be inspired, and learn how to weave God's peacemaking principles and the gospel itself into your life and your church. In doing so, you will position yourself to claim one of the greatest promises in the Bible: "Blessed are the peacemakers, for they will be called the children of God!"

Ken Sande,
founder of Peacemaker Ministries and Relational Wisdom 360

Introduction

*Feeling the Pains That Spoil Unity in Jesus's Church—
the Orlando Grace Story*

Then I said to them, "You see the trouble we are in, how Jerusalem lies
in ruins with its gates burned. Come, let us build the wall of Jerusalem,
that we may no longer suffer derision."

Nehemiah 2:17

The world isn't looking at our tracts and rallies and telecasts and study
manuals. It is looking at us and how we behave. When it fails to see the
unity of Jesus's followers—the church—it fails to see the validation that
Christ is indeed the Son of the living God.

Charles Colson[1]

Sad but true, churches can fight over the silliest—sometimes even
absurd—things. Church consultant Thom Rainer drew such a conclusion in response to a Twitter survey gone viral. He listed twenty-five of
his "favorite" issues from the avalanche of responses. Here's a sample:

An argument over the appropriate length of the worship pastor's
beard.
A church dispute of whether or not to install restroom stall dividers
in the women's restroom.

An argument over the type of filing cabinet to purchase.

A fight over which picture of Jesus to put in the foyer.

An argument over the discovery that the church budget was off by $0.10.

Two different churches reported fights over the type of coffee.

A disagreement over using the term "potluck" instead of "pot blessing."

An argument over who had access to the copy machine.

An argument over whether to have gluten-free communion bread or not.

A fight over whether or not to sing "Happy Birthday" each week.[2]

Sobering list, isn't it? Whether over silly or serious matters, church fights warrant our asking some important questions of ourselves. Deidra Riggs proposes:

> When I watch my brothers and sisters in the body of Christ argue with one another or hear of churches splitting up . . . I have to wonder what's at stake. I wonder what it would take to set up a playdate of sorts so we could try and figure out what common ground might look like. I wonder what answers I might get if I started asking questions like, "What's at stake for you here? Why are you arguing so loudly and calling people names? Why can't we keep worshiping together? . . . What are we clinging to so tightly?"[3]

Our latest church storm—not our first, I'm afraid—rocked us like one of Florida's infamous category-five hurricanes. It left us asking a lot of those questions and others like them. The painful details bear no repeating. With the help of Ken Sande at Peacemaker Ministries, we managed to keep our church version of the *Titanic* from sinking to the bottom.[4] Long story short, in the providence of God, I went from serving as OGC's worship leader to becoming its third lead pastor. I remember asking myself, *Have I lost my mind? Who in the world takes a church with so much wreckage and so troubled a track record? What made me or anyone else in leadership or the church believe that this time would yield different results?*

Admittedly for my own sake, but ultimately for the sake of Jesus's name and the good of the church as well, I pondered these questions and others like them. I searched for answers. I became obsessed with a personal mission. On my watch, however long it might last at OGC, I would do everything I could, with God's help, to see that our church never again suffered such division and despair. I pursued every bit of advanced training I could find on biblical peacemaking.[5] I determined to master what the Bible said about not just how to resolve conflict to the glory of God when it happened but also how to safeguard the unity the God of peace gives his church through his Son, the Prince of Peace.

Now fifteen years into this journey, OGC enjoys, by God's grace and a great deal of informed effort on our part, a culture of peace. We have managed thus far to stay out of any more major troubled waters of conflict. We have seen the Lord weave into our DNA a passion for peace and a warrior-like preserving of the unity that makes us now a healthier-than-ever ministry. We have started moving from a Nehemiah-like "rebuilding the walls" season of recovery to a Jeremiah-like "blessing the city" form of gospel outreach. At age sixty-five, arguably in the fourth quarter of my pastoral ministry career and likely shepherding the last of my churches, I feel burdened and equipped to tell its unique peacemaking story for the good of Christ's church elsewhere.

A number of helpful resources aimed at equipping God's people for resolving church conflict line the bookshelf.[6] Some truly extraordinary authors have contributed their insights to that end. When I teach on peacemaking at our local seminary, I tell the students every time that Ken Sande's book *The Peacemaker* is one of the top five resources in my pastoral toolkit. It comes into play whenever I do conflict coaching and mediation. But *The Peacemaking Church* comes at this gnarly problem of church conflict from a different, absolutely crucial direction. Conflict resolution books take aim at what to do after a meltdown. In other words, they approach things from a *reactive* stance. They are, by design, corrective in nature. And thank God for every single one of them. *The Peacemaking Church* will add a *proactive* approach to your church toolkit. What if the best fight your congregation ever experiences is the one you never get into in the first place? My goal for you and your church in the pages that follow is a fierce passion for excelling in preserving the treasured gift of unity.

God commands many things in his Word that a people gripped by the gospel must embrace in order to bring him glory in the church and in the world. Some of these receive priority attention in terms of requiring an all-in, do-our-best kind of commitment. In chapter 1 of this book, I make the case that peacemaking heads this list. It is absolutely imperative that you adopt this perspective if you are going to do your part in keeping your church out of unnecessary conflict. In part 1, Ephesians 4:1–6 forms the starting place for a perspective of excellence in preserving unity. Chapter 2 introduces the need to see ourselves in the right light as peacemakers. Then chapter 3 moves to making our approach with the right touch in navigating relational challenges. Chapter 4 finishes the all-important perspective with basing our thinking as peacemakers on the right doctrine.

Once we nail down the perspective of our priorities as preservers of unity in the church, part 2 of *The Peacemaking Church* warns about three deadly pitfalls that threaten a church's peace. The world, the flesh, and the devil war against us to jeopardize our oneness and tarnish our testimony in the eyes of the unbelieving community through disunity. The flesh wreaks its particular version of havoc when church members unleash sinful anger in response to offenses that they cannot overlook. Chapter 5 unpacks Jesus's candid warning in Matthew 5 about the risks involved with losing self-control and giving way to rage and his prescription for the peacemaking antidote we need to keep free from judgment for anger and its consequences—even the ultimate kind in hell.

Two other threats to unity are covered in chapters 6 and 7, namely litigating in the courts and judging in the church. Chapter 6 explores Paul's scathing rebuke in 1 Corinthians 6 over Christians taking other Christians to court rather than settling disputes where they belong—within the church. Chapter 7 tackles the challenge of dealing with an all-too-common hindrance to unity among God's people in Romans 14, answering this question: What should Christians do when they disagree over matters of conscience as opposed to clear black-and-white commands of Scripture?

Part 3 of *The Peacemaking Church* focuses on two overarching practices that go a long way to safeguarding unity in Jesus's church. These include an individual and a corporate dimension. For peace to prevail over time, much depends upon the kind of spirit maintained by individuals in the church. Chapter 8 unpacks Abraham's example of relational magnanimity in Genesis 13. His spiritual generosity with his nephew Lot heads off a potential conflict before it ever happens. It represents an ideal template for doing the same in any relationship challenge we face. But in addition to individual responsibilities, corporate commitments come into play as well. Since so many conflicts occur between God's people and the servants he appoints over them as shepherds, chapter 9 deals with 1 Thessalonians 5 and the necessity for followers to esteem their leaders very highly in love. I will show you how to do that in some effective and practical ways.

Whether you are a leader or follower in your church, my aim for you in this book is the same. I want to help turn you into a heavyweight champion of unity in your fellowship. I desire to help you prize oneness for the treasured gift that it is by making its preservation in your church a number one priority. The epilogue concludes on a high note to that end. It comes at things from two angles. Corporately, it extols, from Psalm 133, the delight for God's people when they enjoy unity over a protracted period of time. That kind of blessing brings with it a degree of sweetness so unique that it is worthy of our enthusiastic praise when we gather together for corporate worship. Individually, it speaks, from Matthew 5:9, to the most enviable benefit of earning the title of a *peacemaker* when we act consistently as a peacemaker in the eyes of others.

Before proceeding any further, I have a confession to make. Buckle your seat belt for some major-league irony: days prior to submitting the manuscript for this book to the publisher I—yes I, an aspiring "expert" on this subject just introduced—nearly wrecked the OGC train for the third time in its history. That's right. I shudder to think how perilously close I brought us to the precipice of another churchwide meltdown. Sad, but true. If not for the grace of God *and* the application of principles contained in these pages—I'm not overstating the case here—integrity would have necessitated my abandonment of this project. Here's the deal.

Personally, I've never found pastoral ministry more challenging in my lifetime than at the present. I don't know that I've ever felt less equipped to lead well. I admit all this in the interest of explaining the angst behind poor choices that nearly breached the gates and burned the walls of our ministry yet another time. *Decline* is the best word to describe the situation as of late. Giving is down. Numbers are off. So many families have left our church recently—for good and not-so-good reasons—that I've joked (painfully) about installing a revolving door in the main entryway! As you can imagine, the circumstances have generated a fair amount of conversation within our leadership by way of evaluation. The air I breathe lately often seems heavy with the smog of criticism. It feels unbearable at times. Eventually I let it get to me.

A particular focal point of discussion/concern surrounded our worship and music ministry. Take my word for it. This area of church life—what to sing and play, how to sing and play, who gets to sing and play, when to sing and play—makes particularly fertile ground for sprouting the weeds of church conflict. Fellow pastors, keep your eyes on this baby. It will eat your lunch if you don't watch out.

One fateful elder meeting, we drilled down in this area. Too many "exit interviews" dinged us for various reasons on this front. The consensus seemed plain. Something had to be done. "It's time for a change," as one brother put it. Let me make things perfectly clear: I consented. In spite of gnawing reservations within warning me to push back harder than I did, I ignored them and went with the flow. I and my associate pastor were tasked with breaking the news to the staff couple who had faithfully served in that capacity for years.

Over lunch that following Sunday, we met in my home. I laid out the situation and braced for the backlash I innately knew would follow (I'm not making this whole story up—it really went down this way). Looking back, that critical moment of decision forced upon this couple determined whether we deserved the label "peacemaking church" or not. All I can say is thank God my dear brother and sister put into practice everything this pastor had taught them over the years (their words) and saved the day. They responded magnificently out of regard for the glory of God and the unity of our church. Additionally, they offered some excellent observations as to why the new direction proposed might well prove problematic. More importantly, they pointed out significant leadership/management failures on our part from both a biblical viewpoint and standard business practices. In the end, they asked for a meeting with our elders at the earliest possible convenience to share their hurt and express their concerns. We eagerly granted that request.

As you can imagine, I did some pretty heavy-lifting soul-searching in the meantime. Peacemaking principles, I'm relieved to say, served my own heart well throughout those five agonizing days between meetings. I pleaded with the Lord to take no prisoners in showing me the logs in my own eye (Matt. 7:3–5) contributing to this conflict that—trust me on this assessment—threatened to tear our church apart at the seams. To say the least, I did not like the ugliness revealed.

We had erred on a number of levels. The rebuke in love was deserved. I can't begin to describe the distress I felt at handling the situation so poorly. But something on a deeper heart level disturbed me even more. Why the mismanagement and failure in due process? I can only speak for myself—my main point in sharing this story. For my part, I realized I had panicked. I let a heart idol of needing my church to thrive trump staff loyalty and due process. In my desperation to stop the bleeding and some way—any way—reverse the trend, I managed to put a trusted coworker on the altar of sacrifice. It nearly cost me a treasured friendship. Sometimes the sinfulness of my own heart, graciously revealed by God's doing, makes me shudder in revulsion. But it also drives me to repent and drink again from the fountain of lavish gospel grace.

Our meeting opened that night with my wounded friends reading carefully prepared, measured statements. They spoke the truth in love (Eph. 4:15). We listened to their admonitions and concerns. After they finished, I took the lead on behalf of our elders. I started with, "I botched this," and I finished with, "Will you forgive me?" I wept through most of my "seven A's of confession."[7] I described my failure to lead well, named my heart idol, and owned responsibility as point man for making such a mess. Before I knew it, our chief musician crossed the room and embraced me, saying, "That's the man I know. I forgive you." I wept even harder—tears of joyful relief. We pressed the pause button on our music issues that night. We continue to work on the problem, thankfully with our relationships restored and the church's peace protected. Wow, talk about a close one! We dodged a major bullet with the Lord's help.

I share all that to one end: church unity can be a terribly fragile thing. Even a church and pastor with a self-confessed core value of peacemaking can come dangerously close to losing the battle on the unity front. It takes pastors and people alike committed with bulldog tenacity to nothing short of a do-your-best guarding of church peace. You cannot err in making it too high a priority.

G. K. Chesterton once quipped, "If anything is worth doing, it is worth doing badly."[8] He said that in reference to a defense of hobbies, amateur interests, and various not-so-important pursuits. I am certain he would have considered preserving unity in the church just the opposite—something very much worth doing excellently. Just how well worth doing it is deserves a chapter all its own.

1

Our Best and Nothing Less

Strive for peace with everyone, and for the holiness without which no one will see the Lord.

Hebrews 12:14

Our first and chief concern as Christians should be to guard and to preserve this precious, wondrous unity of the Spirit. . . . If we believe in God, we must ever feel that our first duty is to guard this unity, to preserve it at all costs, to strain every nerve and be diligent in endeavouring to keep it and manifest it.

D. Martyn Lloyd-Jones[1]

Most of us do not just bump into greatness every day. I will never forget one of the rare times I literally did. It happened on a Saturday afternoon at the Norfolk airport. Late for a flight, I hurried into the check-in line. In my haste, I nearly bounced off the 6'7" figure waiting his turn in front of me. As he did a 180 to see who had gotten too close for comfort, I immediately began to beg forgiveness for my clumsiness. But I stopped mid-apology when it dawned on me that I was having a close encounter of the celebrity kind. "Hey, Dr. J!," I said. That's right. I stood face-to-face—or face-to-chest, I should say—with *the* Julius

Erving, NBA legend and Hall of Famer, otherwise known in basketball lore as "The Doctor."

"Hello," he replied, smiling warmly. I proceeded to tell him what a huge fan I was. Now, those of you with admiration for other pro-ball greats and affinity for their teams, please indulge me for a bit. Born and raised in southeast Pennsylvania, I waited a long time for the 76ers to win an NBA title. So when my team finally broke through with a four-game sweep of the perennial champion LA Lakers in the 1982–83 season, I couldn't have been more thrilled. Now, I know the good doctor didn't do it all by himself. A gifted cast of teammates contributed to the success of that memorable season. But few basketball aficionados would dispute that Julius Erving led the way to the only Larry O'Brien trophy in Philadelphia history. I wanted Dr. J to know just how grateful I was to him for making that possible. I scored his autograph (for my sons, of course), and off we went to the gate. I could hardly believe what had just happened.

No doubt about it, I credit Julius Erving for his extraordinary contribution to my team's place in the NBA record books. But the man commands my admiration and that of many others for another reason, a more compelling one, at least in terms of what I do for a living. They called Julius Erving "Dr. J," or "The Doctor," for good reason. Any basketball lover from that generation knows why. All you had to do was watch him "operate" on the court. From his patented finger-roll touch to his soaring flight from the top of the key to throwing down a thunderous dunk, Number 6 made folks gasp with awe by the way he performed round-ball surgery on his opponents. Whether history's best or not (I too have heard of Michael Jordan, Magic Johnson, Larry Bird, LeBron James, and Steph Curry, just to name a few), Dr. J belongs in the category of all-time greats who did it better than most and belong to a league apart from the rest.

Now, nobody cares in the least how well I do or do not perform on a basketball court. That's a good thing. I have never been much of an athlete. But every member of my church cares greatly about how I do in the pulpit as their lead pastor. My job description in that role at Orlando Grace Church includes a number of responsibilities, but none more important than preaching God's Word every Sunday. It matters greatly to me that I approach my vocation as a teacher of the Bible for God's people with something of the devotion and excellence exhibited by the likes of an All-Star athlete in his vocation.

Furthermore, I really don't have any choice in the matter. I've got to go hard after excellence in my realm for multiple reasons. The apostle Paul spelled out the most obvious of those in 2 Timothy 2:15. Speaking to his young pastoral protégé serving the church at Ephesus, he urged: "Do your best to present yourself to God as one approved, a worker who has no need to be ashamed, rightly handling the word of truth." *Do your best.* Here's how this pastor feels the weight of those words every time he reads them:

> Hold nothing back. Give your all. Study hard. Wrestle with the text. Spend the time. Labor super well. Pay the price in blood, sweat, and tears during sermon prep to ensure you get the meaning spot-on. Be the best you can be at this preaching thing. After all, ultimately it's God's "Well done, good and faithful servant" approval you seek to receive more than anything else. Or it should be. No way you want to cut corners here as a pastor, that's for sure. Shame on you if you do!

Bible verses like these can keep preachers like me awake at night. We wonder if we are coming anywhere close to what God requires, given a bar set so high. My fellow pastors reading this will likely identify. But what does that have to do with everyone else hanging in there with me thus far?

Here's my point. God's Word tells not just pastors but all believers many things we must *do* for Jesus in light of who we *are* in Jesus. But, as with pastors in their unique role, the Bible charges *all* believers with a select list of responsibilities subject to a "be the best we can be, give our all, go all-out" kind of devotion. We don't want to be ashamed in the least about these crucial matters. One of those responsibilities in particular for every church-going follower of Jesus gets a lot of Bible press. I'm talking about peacemaking. The Scriptures make this very clear in numerous places. Perhaps Ephesians 4:1–6 says it most thoroughly:

> I therefore, a prisoner for the Lord, urge you to walk in a manner worthy of the calling to which you have been called, with all humility and gentleness, with patience, bearing with one another in love, eager to maintain the unity of the Spirit in the bond of peace. There is one body and one Spirit—just as you were called to the one hope that belongs to your call—one Lord, one faith, one baptism, one God and Father of all, who is over all and through all and in all.

Camp out with me for a moment on that word *eager* in verse 3. Paul argues that a life gripped by the gospel of Jesus will, among other things, demonstrate itself in an eagerness for keeping the peace in the body of Christ. The word for *eager* in the original text is the same word translated "do your best" in 2 Timothy 2:15. It shows up again in 2 Peter 1:5–7, translated a bit differently but conveying a similar idea, included in a list of highly desirable virtues in a believer's life:

> For this very reason, *make every effort* to supplement your faith with virtue, and virtue with knowledge, and knowledge with self-control, and self-control with steadfastness, and steadfastness with godliness, and godliness with brotherly affection, and brotherly affection with love. (emphasis added)

Be eager. Do your best. Make every effort. These are multiple ways of saying virtually the same thing. They all capture the verb's urgency regardless of the subject under consideration. The Greek word comes from a root that means to run or make haste, to hurry about something. It communicates the idea of speed, urgency, energy—a vigorous pursuit of something. Theologian Markus Barth nailed it with his assessment of this word, so important to each of these contexts:

> It is hardly possible to render exactly the urgency contained in the underlying Greek verb. Not only haste and passion, but a full effort of the whole man is meant, involving his will, sentiment, reason, physical strength, and total attitude. The imperative mood of the participle found in the Greek text excludes passivity, quietism, a wait-and-see attitude, or a diligence tempered by all deliberate speed. Yours is the initiative! Do it now! Mean it! *You* are to do it! I mean it!—Such are the overtones in verse 3.[2]

Paul commands that this is the way we should regard the call to peacemaking for unity's sake in the body of Christ. Allow me to pile on the emphasis with a few more imperatives in the New Testament.

> Strive for peace with everyone, and for the holiness without which no one will see the Lord. (Heb. 12:14)

> If possible, so far as it depends on you, live peaceably with all. (Rom. 12:18)

So then let us pursue what makes for peace and for mutual upbuilding. (Rom. 14:19)

How can we possibly miss the point? Nothing less than our very best will suffice when it comes to safeguarding unity in Jesus's church as far as it depends upon us.

Let me ask you a question: What's something you want very much to do well? I mean, you really, really, really desire to excel in it. When it comes to that particular skill or interest, it matters to you that you do your very best—you give it all you've got—particularly in the church. Do you have the gift of teaching? I'll bet you work very hard at your study and lesson prep for the good of your students. Do you play or sing on the church's music team? No doubt you give lots of time to rehearsal in getting ready for the worship services. What about nursery care, greeting, hospitality, small group leading, and all sorts of other important tasks it takes to make churches function to the glory of God and the joy of their people? I can scarcely imagine that most servants do not care a great deal about doing a consistently good, if not first-rate, job, whatever their assignment for Jesus. Or at least they should!

So, here's the deal. Do you think that way in terms of your role as a peacemaker in your church? Do you consider the call to guard the unity and peace of your body of believers as something you take so seriously that it gets your absolute best in terms of prayer, energy, strategy, and overall commitment? How far up your ladder of church concerns do you rank preserving the unity of the Spirit in the bond of peace? If I correctly understand the Bible's gist of things on this subject, you will want to bump this to the top of the list immediately, if it doesn't already enjoy an A-Priority standing in your estimation. If you are going to be eager about anything in your church, let it be this.

I love to hunt. I used to live in north/central Idaho, and I still own a five-acre bit of paradise at the base of the Clearwater Mountains. I travel back there whenever I can for some R&R. There are few things I look forward to more than the opening of white-tailed deer and elk season every October. Each evening just before dusk, my good friend Dick and I grab our rifles and walk the hills behind our little town. We are men on a mission. We comb those woods and stalk the fields. We've got one aim in mind—to locate the biggest rack we can, bag it, and tag it. (My apologies to Bambi lovers everywhere.) I can't tell you

23

how eager I am to do that every fall. I think about it year round. And that's precisely the kind of zeal that should characterize our pursuit of peace in the church.

Before closing this chapter with a view to where we go from here, I want to pay tribute to quite possibly the best peacemaker I've ever known, my wife Nancy. She and I were married for nearly forty-two years, and she went home to Jesus in May 2016 after an eighteen-month battle with ovarian cancer. Nan took Ephesians 4:1–3 seriously in the church and in our marriage. She eagerly preserved the unity of the Spirit in the bond of peace. She embraced the blessedness Jesus promised in Matthew 5:9. She decidedly deserved the label "child of God."

In the context of our marriage especially, Nancy excelled in ten practical qualities of a peacemaker that apply to any context. Here's a ten-point reality checklist by which to measure your own commitment as a prize peacemaker.

One, she loved Jesus more than she loved me (Matt. 10:37–39). From the day of her conversion, Nan counted the costs of discipleship. The Lord was first in her affections. She knew it was not wise to pursue her soul's satisfaction in me. God never made any spouse or other human being fit for a task only he can accomplish (Ps. 37:4).

Two, she chose not to allow me to control her joy quotient (1 Thess. 5:16–18). She had to learn this over time, but she got there. In conflict she came to distinguish the difference between what was about me and what was about her. And when it was about me—and it often was— she released and rested in Jesus. Only one Person should have control over a believer's emotional condition. His name is the Holy Spirit (Gal. 5:22–23).

Three, she perfected the art of asking me questions (Prov. 20:5). Nancy got me big-time on this. She knew if she outright challenged something I thought, said, or did, I could easily get defensive (again, that's on me). She consistently helped draw out my heart with strategic questions that facilitated conversation toward oneness. In so doing she kept respect for me high while still making her point. I loved this about her! She engaged my heart; she didn't stomp all over it. (See chapter 5 on anger for more on this important peacemaking skill.)

Four, she refused worrisome nagging, choosing rather to wait on God for change in me (Prov. 21:19). It's not that Nancy wouldn't say hard things to me. I assure you, she knew how to shoot straight with me (see number six below). But once she made her case, she let things rest—asking the Lord to do in my heart what only he could do (Isa. 40:27–31).

Five, she didn't do what I call peacebreaking (Prov. 15:18). Some will question my memory on this. It is true just the same. Nan lost her cool with me only one time in all our years together. Only once! Isn't that remarkable? And as I recall, I definitely deserved it. Outbursts of anger crush oneness. We simply refused to go there by God's grace.

Six, she also didn't do what I call peacefaking (Eph. 4:25–27). Sorry to say, I specialized in stuffing my anger and punishing Nan with the cold shoulder treatment. (More on that in chapter 5 as well.) Thankfully, I got better about this over time, but Nan never struggled with fear of conflict issues like I did. She consistently told it like it was in love.

Seven, she overlooked my sin—a lot (Prov. 19:11). Nan outright forgave me for my offenses over and over again without saying a word. *She was not easily offended.* This matters so much to both marital oneness and church oneness. (More on this crucial virtue in chapter 3.)

Eight, she consistently forgave me for my sins (Eph. 4:32). Nancy lived out the gospel of grace by showing her foremost-of-sinners husband (1 Tim. 1:15) forgiving grace. She practiced the four promises of forgiveness—especially never using the past as a weapon against me.[3] Good grief, I was a fortunate man! If you only knew.

Nine, she embraced assisted peacemaking with me when necessary (Matt. 18:15–18; Phil. 4:2–3).[4] We visited a fair number of Christian counselors over the years. We could barely afford the cost for counseling. But the way we saw it, we couldn't afford *not* to get with a trained professional. Somehow the Lord always provided, and we never regretted the investment. If we got stuck with maintaining oneness, we got help restoring oneness.

Ten, she never wavered on her covenant commitments (Matt. 5:37). Her yes was yes and her no was no. On December 21, 1974, then-Nancy Masologites spoke vows to me, Curtis Heffelfinger. She promised to love and to cherish, for richer or poorer, in sickness and in health, for better or for worse, until death did us part. Death did part us in 2016, but Nancy's legacy lives on in so many ways—including in my aim to be a better peacemaking man and pastor for the rest of my days on the planet.

That's my aim for every reader who picks up and stays with *The Peacemaking Church*. I want to help make you a better peacemaking person whatever the context. So, what more does that look like? A thorough unpacking of Paul's line of thinking in Ephesians 4:1–6 makes an essential starting place. It reveals three priorities believers must embrace to earn a superior rating in the "resolving conflict" and "preserving unity" categories of church life:

Priority #1: Seeing ourselves as peacemakers in the right light.

Priority #2: Shaping our approach as peacemakers with the right touch.

Priority #3: Basing our thinking as peacemakers on the right doctrine.

Packaged together, these three priorities, lived out by the majority of folks in any given congregation, leaders and followers alike, will go a long way to helping them stay out of troublesome and often excruciatingly painful conflict. Remember what I said in the introduction? The best church fight is the one your church never gets into in the first place. It all starts with the way we grasp our identity as peacemakers, Paul's first concern in the fourth chapter of his letter to the church at Ephesus.

PART ONE

Embracing the Priorities That Preserve Unity in Jesus's Church

2

Seeing Ourselves as Peacemakers in the Right Light

Walk in a manner worthy of the calling to which you have been called.

Ephesians 4:1

Perspective is everything when you are experiencing the challenges of life.

Joni Eareckson Tada[1]

In his book *Great Church Fights*, Leslie Flynn quotes the following news story about a feud in a Welsh church looking for a new pastor:

Yesterday the two opposition groups both sent ministers to the pulpit. Both spoke simultaneously, each trying to shout above the other. Both called for hymns, and the congregation sang two—each side trying to drown out the other. Bibles were raised in anger. The Sunday morning service turned into bedlam. Through it all, the two preachers continued to outshout each other with their sermons. Eventually, a deacon called a policeman. Two came in and began shouting for the congregation to be quiet. They advised the 40 persons in the church to return home. The rivals filed out, still arguing. Last night one of the groups called a "let's be friends" meeting. It broke up in argument.[2]

Obviously those folks did not get the Ephesians 4:1–6 memo about doing one's best in safeguarding unity in Jesus's church!

Before digging into the details Paul prescribes in Ephesians 4, remember that this book, along with Galatians, Philippians, and Colossians, is one of what we call Paul's prison epistles in the New Testament. He likely wrote it in Rome while bound with chains. It is one of the grandest of Paul's letters, treating some of the most magnificent themes of the Christian faith. It contains a very familiar structure common to a number of the apostle's writings. He starts with a doctrinal section—the indicative—who we are in Christ, and then moves to a practical section—the imperative—what we should do for Christ as a result. For Paul, doctrine always informed duty. You can see that structure very clearly in Ephesians. The doctrinal section spans chapters 1–3. Then in chapter 4, signaled by the pivotal word *therefore* in verse 1, he shifts gears to the practical. He moves from information to application, from description to prescription.

A Worthy Walk

Along with the word *therefore* in verse 1, we have a favorite word picture Paul used in his writings: walking. It doubly alerts us that we have moved past what we should know in our heads about God to how we should actually live our lives for God. "Walk in a manner worthy of the calling to which you have been called" (Eph. 4:1). We use the same word picture when we say something like, "She walks her talk." It is a way of referencing the whole tenor of someone's conduct, the way she handles herself, the manner of her everyday lifestyle.

Paul pleads in the most passionate of ways at the outset of chapter 4. In light of everything revealed in the first half of his letter, he entreats his readers to live out the implications of those truths in a worthy kind of lifestyle. Now, please don't miss this. I want you to make the connection with where Paul immediately goes from this overarching word picture of a worthy walk: peacemaking! He dives headlong into a challenging list of relational virtues (more on those in chapter 3). But for now let it sink in where he lands that list with these words in verse 3: "eager to maintain the unity of the Spirit in the bond of peace." That will remain his thrust all the way to verse 16.

Not until verse 17 does Paul transition to talking about a worthy walk with a second and different specific application—personal purity. You might think he would have started there. But he did not. He launches the application section of the letter with the necessity of preserving unity within the body of Christ *before* he tackles a call to individual holiness. This communicates a great deal about just how high a priority this peacemaking emphasis must be for believers. Not that individual holiness is second class. Of course not. But, for reasons related to themes he addresses in Ephesians 2 and 3, Paul concentrates initially on the priority of preserving unity before anything else. Larry Richards and Clyde Hoeldtke explain:

> In Jesus, persons with great racial and social differences, which had caused deep hostility, have been made one. In the one body, Christ has made peace, reconciling us to God and each other and ending the hostility (2:14–18). This supernatural act that has made us one body has also made us sharers in the promise of Jesus, and in that great miracle of unity the complex wisdom of God will be eternally revealed to all created beings (3:6–11).
>
> Because we are one, we are urged to build intimate relationships with each other. . . . In this way we are to "make every effort to keep the unity of the Spirit through the bond of peace" (4:1–6).[3]

Conclusion? A life consistent with Jesus's glorious calling strives to safeguard the treasure of unity in Christ's church. This is Priority One of a worthy walk in Jesus. In the rest of this chapter, let's look at the first of the three priorities Paul prescribes for gospel-shaped guardians of unity: seeing ourselves as peacemakers in the right light—captive and called.

Prisoner for the Lord

Right out of the chute, Paul calls himself "a prisoner for the Lord" (4:1). He has done the same once before in this letter: "For this reason, I, Paul, a prisoner of Christ Jesus on behalf of you Gentiles" (3:1). He likely means the term both literally and figuratively. As already noted, Paul actually wrote while under house arrest in Rome. He had been imprisoned for believing and teaching what he expounded in chapters

1–3. That's how completely dedicated he was to those realities. For him they were worth every bit of suffering he endured.

But I agree with Eileen Rife in detecting undertones to this phrase that run deeper than simply the literal meaning. She writes:

> Other places in Scripture, Paul refers to himself as a bondslave of the Lord [see Rom. 1:1]. Here in Ephesians . . . he says I am the prisoner of Christ Jesus. A common theme runs throughout Paul's life. . . . Paul sees himself as a prisoner of Christ Jesus because he has already surrendered to Christ's lordship in his life. He is not bound by the Romans, any more than Jesus was nailed to the cross by the Romans. He is bound by loyalty to and love for the One He faithfully serves.[4]

The prisoner metaphor conveys an important concept. This is the way we have to view ourselves when it comes to maintaining unity in the church when something or someone threatens to disrupt it. Those who strive for excellence in peacemaking—they always aim to do their best—start by seeing themselves as *captives* of Jesus and his will when it comes to this all-important priority. It is not negotiable for them. They simply will not take it or leave it. They have received a command from King Jesus, captain of their salvation: be eager—a present-tense imperative, to "keep on being, always be eager" as Barth pointed out—to maintain the unity of the Spirit in the bond of peace.

Every September at Orlando Grace we observe what I call "Conciliation Anniversary Sunday." I lead us to recall our last great church fight back in 2002. We give thanks to God for the remarkable way He has worked all things together for our good (Rom. 8:28). I always preach on a passage emphasizing peacemaking in one way or another. That annual service is an important way we seek to safeguard our unity and avoid a future meltdown. One other component makes its way into the order of service that day. We recite The Peacemaker Pledge. I particularly like the reminder at the end:

> By God's grace, we will apply these principles as a matter of stewardship, realizing that *conflict is an opportunity* [to honor God, love others, and grow in Christlikeness] *not an accident*. We will remember that success in God's eyes is not a matter of specific results, but of faithful, dependent obedience.[5]

And when Jesus, the commander and chief, gives one of his own the assignment of peacemaking, what should he do? He should embrace it, go hard after it, do his best to complete the task, as far as it depends on him, because he grasps his identity—prisoner for the Lord. He is bound by his allegiance to Jesus to do what pleases him no matter how difficult the task.

Called by the Lord

Seeing ourselves as peacemakers in the right light involves one other crucial perspective. After identifying himself as a prisoner for the Lord in Ephesians 4:1, Paul admonishes, "Walk in a manner worthy of the calling to which you have been called." If we are going to excel as peacemaking people in the church, we need to see ourselves not just as captive to Jesus as his "prisoners" to do his bidding; we also need to see ourselves as his "called" people. This calling thing is huge for Paul. You can tell by the way he keeps coming back to it. He has already prayed about it on their behalf, asking, "that you may know what is the hope to which he has called you" (Eph. 1:18). He refers to it again in the context of chapter 4. "There is one body and one Spirit—just as you were called to the one hope that belongs to your call" (4:4).

Now what is he talking about? Two cross-references give us some help. Paul includes this concept of calling in what is sometimes referred to as the Golden Chain of Salvation: "And those whom he predestined he also called, and those whom he called he also justified, and those whom he justified he also glorified" (Rom. 8:30). In 2 Timothy 1:9 Paul references the same thing again, speaking of God "who saved us and called us to a holy calling, not because of our works but because of his own purpose and grace, which he gave us in Christ Jesus before the ages began." The Bible refers to different kinds of calling. But here, and in Ephesians, Paul has in mind what scholars label "the effective call." Theologian Wayne Grudem defines it this way: "Effective calling is an act of God the Father, speaking through the human proclamation of the gospel, in which he summons people to himself in such a way that they respond in saving faith."[6] It is the sovereign voice of God that brings a person dead in trespasses and sin to be alive with Christ in spiritual birth (Eph. 2:1–6).

One New Man in Place of the Two

In Ephesians 1 and 2 Paul unpacks two aspects of this glorious salvation calling. There are individual aspects as well as certain corporate aspects to it. We are not just saved and blessed as individuals with every spiritual blessing in Christ; we are called and saved into a community. There, divisions and distinctions, particularly in Paul's day between Jew and Gentile, have been broken down. Here's how he puts it in Ephesians 2:13–16.

> But now in Christ Jesus you who once were far off have been brought near by the blood of Christ. For he himself is our peace, who has made us both one and has broken down in his flesh the dividing wall of hostility by abolishing the law of commandments expressed in ordinances, that he might create in himself one new man in place of the two, so making peace, and might reconcile us both to God in one body through the cross, thereby killing the hostility.

This is why Paul frames things the way he does when he commands, "Maintain the unity of the Spirit in the bond of peace" (4:3). Our calling as believers is to *maintain* the priceless reality of unity that the Holy Spirit has already given. The idea behind the word is to keep or guard church oneness like you would a treasure—even for those most hostile toward one another like Jews and Gentiles were in the first century. God's peace is a bond that cements even the most different and diverse peoples together so that they can safeguard this gift *already* entrusted to the church.

Timothy Lane and Paul Tripp connect the cause-and-effect dots perfectly in their excellent book *How People Change*:

> In light of the great grace of God, Paul calls members of this new community to enter into relationships with their Christian brothers and sisters in humility, gentleness, patience, and forbearance. He urges the church to be vigilant to keep the unity of the Spirit; *he does not tell them to create it, because it is already a fact*. When you trust in Christ, you are immediately welcomed into fellowship with the source of love, the triune God, and with his family, the church. In light of that, spare no effort to make sure your relationships reflect the unity and love of Father, Son, and Holy Spirit. It all begins, continues, and will end with God at the center. (emphasis added)[7]

So we can really boil down these opening verses of Ephesians 4 to this idea: the church truly *is* spiritually one by Jesus's saving grace, so let it *be* spiritually one with his supernatural help. The first three chapters of Ephesians describe what Jesus has accomplished in his decisive work of atonement on the cross. He has broken down every wall of hostility between peoples. Through the Holy Spirit he effectively makes them one in a bond of peace. Where Paul takes his readers now is how to maintain that through excellence in peacemaking. But it is altogether important that we start our way of thinking about excelling in peacemaking right here: get a grip on your identity. You are captive for Christ as peacemakers and called in Christ for peacemaking.

I recall an occasion where this issue of embracing our identity seemed especially applicable at our church. One year on our conciliation anniversary Sunday, I preached from Matthew 6:14–15. The context contains the Lord's Prayer. After unpacking six specific petitions in verses 9–13 as a game plan for shaping the content of our praying, the Lord adds verses 14 and 15 as an appendix of sorts related to the fifth of the requests. The petition itself is familiar for sure: "Forgive us our debts, as we also have forgiven our debtors" (Matt. 6:12). R. C. Sproul comments, emphasizing the latter half of the verse: "That's one of the most frightening lines in the Lord's Prayer. If this condition is to be taken literally, we are finished."[8] It might be one of the most frightening lines in the entire Bible, for that matter. Given the stakes, it should give us the willies no matter how we spin it. But it gets even scarier before Jesus finishes, because he adds a postscript to that request. None of the other five get the same treatment. I think the Lord emphasizes the forgiveness piece in prayer to hammer home the inherent risks attached to an unforgiving spirit. It reads like this:

> For if you forgive others their trespasses, your heavenly Father will also forgive you, but if you do not forgive others their trespasses, neither will your Father forgive your trespasses. (vv. 14–15)

Some sermons generate more responses than others. That one stirred up stuff in more hearts than usual.

A few weeks later, one of our members approached me after a service looking for counsel. He informed me that he had a peacemaking question fostered by that forgiveness message. It convicted him. While guarding confidentiality by not naming the other person involved, he described a breakdown in a relationship with another brother who was also a covenant member. They had already attempted personal peacemaking, but to no avail. Eventually the other man decided that they needed to drop things and essentially have nothing to do with each other. They still came to the same church but avoided one another on Sundays. They even sat on opposite sides of a Sunday school room so they didn't have to engage. I remember thinking, *Even in a church that espouses a high peacemaking value, we still have such a long way to go.* I also made a mental note that we couldn't emphasize this value enough. People struggle so much with resolving conflict well that we have to continually cast a vision for excellence in peacemaking and use every platform we can—sermons, blog posts, social media, newsletters, counseling, and personal conversations. It's virtually impossible to overemphasize this crucial area of church life.

Let's get back to the response to the forgiveness sermon. In a desire to be a doer of the Word and not just a hearer only (James 1:22–25), my grief-stricken sheep decided to reach out again to his fellow member in pursuit of reconciliation. Once more he met with resistance. Now, again, we teach assisted peacemaking around here—seeking the help of a mediator or arbitrators when personal peacemaking efforts fail. So he pressed in, asking, "Could we meet with Pastor Curt to get his help with working out our differences?" Same response: "No, I won't meet with you and PC" (my nickname around OGC).

Granted, I had only heard one side of the story. One thing I've learned in hours of conflict coaching and mediation ministry is that it is vital to work both sides of the street. You can't get anything near a complete picture of the situation without hearing out all parties. But for the life of me, I was baffled at the logjam. Here's where the identity component as peacemakers fits in. If I had the opportunity to hear the other brother's story, at some point I would have wanted to turn him to Ephesians 4:1 and ask, "Do you see yourself as a prisoner of the Lord, held captive to do his will? Do you acknowledge, as a follower of Jesus, that he has called you to a glorious calling? Can you connect the dots with me from the Scriptures here that, as called and captive of the Lord, the way you walk with him as a peacemaker matters greatly to him? If so, wouldn't that necessitate consenting to this repeated plea to work out the conflict? Wouldn't eagerness to preserve unity warrant going the extra mile in this situation? How can the present MO of avoidance and self-protection honor God and advance earnest love for one another (1 Pet. 4:8)?"

If we don't see ourselves in this all-important light, we are much more likely to duck our peacemaking assignments rather than embrace them. Pastors, help your people see this fundamental identity shaped by the gospel. Remind your folks often about it. When you confront somebody who balks at doing their best at peacemaking, get their nose in this text and help them get it! It can be painstaking and time- and labor-intensive work, but sheep need their shepherd's patient, coaching help to do their best at preserving unity in the church (2 Tim. 2:24–26). The truth of God's Word is powerful to effect change in the hearts and lives of the Lord's people (Heb. 4:12).

At one point while writing this chapter, something dawned on me. I'm advocating the importance of embracing an identity in Jesus as a peacemaker, yet absolutely nothing about how "Curt Heffelfinger" self-identifies on social media reflects that in his profile. I decided to fix things immediately on my Twitter account—@revheff. Wanting to practice what I preach, I revised my site to read this way:

> Disciple and beloved son of King Jesus, servant, **peacemaker**, husband, father, grandfather, lead pastor at Orlando Grace Church, blogger, and author.

Do you tweet? Join me and maybe we will start a new trend!

Church historian Theodoret, in his work *Ecclesiastical History*, documents the account of Saint Telemachus, a fifth-century monk. The story has morphed into a variety of forms over the centuries, one even told by then-president Ronald Reagan at the 1984 National Prayer Breakfast. Theodoret's account goes like this:

> Honorius, who had received the empire of Europe, abolished the an-cient exhibitions of gladiators in Rome on the following occasion. A certain man named Telemachus, who had embraced a monastical life, came from the East to Rome at a time when these cruel spectacles were being exhibited. After gazing upon the combat from the amphitheater,

he descended into the arena, and tried to separate the gladiators. The sanguinary spectators, possessed by the demon who delights in the effusion of blood, were irritated at the interruption of their cruel sports, and stoned him who had occasioned the cessation. When being apprised of this circumstance, the admirable emperor numbered him with the victorious martyrs, and abolished these iniquitous spectacles.[9]

Typically the story gets told with Telemachus crying out three times, as he stepped between the combatants, "In the name of Christ, forbear!" Now, I can't confirm the truth of that. It is not in Theodoret's history. But I ask you, what else would possess a man to risk all and ultimately give everything for peacemaking on such a horrendous stage except the name of Christ as one captive to him and called by him? I can think of nothing else adequate for such a challenge.

Jesus Christ descended into a different gladiatorial arena on a hill called Calvary about two thousand years ago to face the same devil who delights in the effusion of blood. That contest to end all contests Paul describes in Colossians 2:13–15.

And you, who were dead in your trespasses and the uncircumcision of your flesh, God made alive together with him, having forgiven us all our trespasses, by canceling the record of debt that stood against us with its legal demands. This he set aside, nailing it to the cross. He disarmed the rulers and authorities and put them to open shame, by triumphing over them in him.

Are you his captive? Have you responded to his calling? I assume many readers of a book like this likely already have a personal relationship with Jesus. But if that might not be true in your case, I want to invite you to respond to Christ today. You can be set free from slavery to sin, Satan, and guilt by repenting of your sins that condemn you and putting your faith in Jesus, who will save you. You will become his captive, forgiven and free. You will belong to his body. And as captive and called, you will inherit a sacred stewardship: safeguarding the unity of the Spirit in the bond of peace.

Follower of Jesus—adjust your view of self accordingly—captive and called for the cause of peace in the church of Jesus Christ. It makes a world of difference in the way you personally conduct yourself, especially when conflict threatens to disrupt your church's treasured peace.

3

Shaping Our Approach as Peacemakers with the Right Touch

Let your reasonableness be known to everyone. The Lord is at hand.

Philippians 4:5

Many years ago I was driven to the conclusion that the two major causes of most emotional problems among evangelical Christians are these: the failure to understand, receive, and live out God's unconditional grace and forgiveness, and the failure to give out that unconditional love, forgiveness, and grace to other people. . . . Many of us are like that. We read, we hear, we believe a good theology of grace. But that's not the way we live. We believe grace in our heads but not in our gut level feelings or in our relationships.

David Seamands[1]

"Mr. Heffelfinger, there's no easy way to say this: you have cancer. Get to treatment yesterday." Those words, spoken in 2005 by an oral surgeon about a fast-growing, killer tumor on the right side of my tongue, set in motion a furious campaign to save my life. Before hearing the "all clear," I endured the big three: surgery, radiation, and chemotherapy. Gratefully, God used all of it to give me length of days and keep me preaching, albeit minus 30 percent of my tongue.

Any survivor will tell you—the C word changes your life forever. Quite the tutor, cancer. I would never voluntarily sign up for it again, but I would not trade its lessons for anything. Among them? What a difference it makes when a doctor employs just the right bedside manner. My oncologist modeled an approach with his patients that made me want to come out a better pastor on the other side of cancer treatment. Dr. G had no problem shooting straight with me when I needed it. He told me more than once, "We sent you to hell and back to save your life." But never once did he demonstrate anything less than the kindest, most compassionate, and gentlest of demeanors along the way. Most of us have heard horror stories about doctors schooled in the Marquis de Sade curriculum of bedside manner. Not my Dr. G.

Many of us in the body of Christ could learn a thing or two from someone like my oncologist. Our failures in this regard indict us saved-by-grace types. Philip Yancey rightly challenged our shortcomings with questions like these: "If grace is so amazing, why don't Christians show more of it? How is it that Christians called to dispense the aroma of grace instead emit the noxious fumes of ungrace?"[2] If we want to make more than a passing grade as peacemakers, we must confront this dilemma head-on. Preserving unity is not just about seeing ourselves in the right light—captive and called as peacemakers—as important as that is. It also has a great deal to do with the way we navigate relationships in the church—redolent with love and grace.

In Ephesians 4:2–3, Paul lists five virtues that are absolutely necessary if we are to qualify as excelling in preserving unity in the body of Christ. The ESV lists them as humility, gentleness, patience, forbearance, and eagerness. Embraced and applied in our lives through the Spirit's help, they combine to shape an approach to relating to other Christians readily described as laced with grace. It is the kind of thing Paul commends when he exhorts, "Let your reasonableness be known to everyone" (Phil. 4:5). Similarly he exhorts, "Let your speech always be gracious" (Col. 4:6). As we work through these five virtues, ask the Lord to help you evaluate your own life realistically in terms of their challenging requirements.

All Humility

Not just humility, mind you. That word is tough enough to swallow all by itself. But Paul had to go and modify it with the word "all" at the beginning of verse 2. Why did he have to add that word? I struggle enough with pride. Did he really have to pile on the pressure with a word like *all*? He left no wiggle room for my arrogance whatsoever. Culturally speaking, Paul's starting place here was unusual. The Greeks never used this word for humility in a favorable sense. It always carried negative connotations. Imagine an abject, servile, cowering slave, and you will get the picture. Not until Jesus came on the scene would anyone use this word positively to describe himself. But Jesus did in Matthew 11:28–29, in a rare comment of self-description:

> Come to me, all who labor and are heavy laden, and I will give you rest. Take my yoke upon you, and learn from me, for I am gentle and *lowly* in heart, and you will find rest for your souls. (emphasis added)

Jesus's word "lowly" is the very same Greek word Paul uses in Ephesians 4:2 that we translate as "humility."

Things haven't changed much today, have they? As a rule, in our culture humility does not get high marks as a quality for getting ahead. But if we determine to excel as peacemakers, we must take our cue from Jesus and start right here. I suspect Paul does so because, if we get this, the remaining virtues in the list will likely flow much more readily from our hearts into our practice of community.

The New Testament emphasizes this all-important unity-preserving virtue of humility elsewhere:

> Do nothing from selfish ambition or conceit, but in humility count others more significant than yourselves. Let each of you look not only to his own interests, but also to the interests of others. (Phil. 2:3–4)

> Put on then, as God's chosen ones, holy and beloved, compassionate hearts, kindness, humility, meekness, and patience. (Col. 3:12)

> Finally, all of you, have unity of mind, sympathy, brotherly love, a tender heart, and a humble mind. (1 Pet. 3:8)

Likewise, you who are younger, be subject to the elders. Clothe your-selves, all of you, with humility toward one another, for "God opposes the proud but gives grace to the humble." (1 Pet. 5:5)

Of course it is one thing to acknowledge the priority of humility in our relationships. No problem there. But it is quite another thing for us actually to master humility's demands in getting along in Jesus's church. Puritan Thomas Watson (1620–86) offered this prescription:

> A humble man values others at a higher rate than himself, and the reason is because he can see his own heart better than he can another's. He sees his own corruption and thinks surely it is not so with others; their graces are not so weak as his; their corruptions are not so strong. "Surely," he thinks, "they have better hearts than I." A humble Christian studies his own infirmities and another's excellences and that makes him put a higher value upon others than himself. "Surely I am more brutish than any man" (Prov. 30:2).[3]

Paul would no doubt venture a loud "Amen!" After all, in his own words, "Christ Jesus came into the world to save sinners, of whom I am the foremost" (1 Tim. 1:15). Maintaining a sobering perspective like Watson's goes a long way in keeping "all humility" the tenor of grace-shaped relationships. But America's great theologian Jonathan Edwards (1703–1758) argued for a comparison even more significant than ourselves with others, if we ever hope to come close to the "all humility" Paul demands of keepers of the peace in Jesus's church:

> Humility doth primarily, and chiefly consist in *a sense of our mean-ness as compared with God,* or a sense of the infinite distance there is between God and ourselves. . . . There is no true humility without somewhat of this spirit; for, however sensible we may be of our mean-ness as compared with some of our fellow creatures, we are not truly humble unless we have a sense of our nothingness as compared with God. . . . And if we are ignorant of our meanness as compared with him, then the most essential thing, and that which is indispensable in true humility, is wanting.[4]

It pains me to confess something. But I fear it presents an occupa-tional hazard for every pastor. For way too long in my ministry I—and my people—suffered from a massive blind spot of pride in my life. Paul's words in Romans 12:3—"I say to everyone among you not to think of himself more highly than he ought to think"—might as well have been cut out of my Bible. Early on in my ministry I majored exceptionally well in entertaining an overinflated view of my self-importance. I lost my first church over a health battle with chronic fatigue syndrome. Before accepting the inevitable with the leadership, I lobbied for an unpaid leave of absence in hopes of retaining the position. In a meeting with my associate pastor and board chairman to discuss the situation, I boasted in a way that still makes me shudder with embarrassment whenever I think of it. I argued for keeping me by asserting something like, "Besides, you will have a hard time finding somebody else out there with the same gifts and abilities I possess."

No, I'm not making that up. I really said it. Sad, yes? The leave was granted. It lasted six months before I succumbed to the illness and resigned. A few years later, the Lord lowered the boom on my hubris and I repented. That involved going back to those brothers and asking their forgiveness for my prideful boasting, which they graciously granted.

Recently I've been rereading Paul Tripp's book *Dangerous Calling*. He tackles head-on risks for pastors such as pride, and he offers helpful counsel that is important to understand:

> I always say it this way: "No one is more influential in your life than you are, because no one talks to you more than you do." Whether you realize it or not, you are in an unending conversation with yourself, and the things you say to you about you are formative of the way you live. You are constantly talking to yourself about your identity, your spirituality, your functionality, your emotionality, your mentality, your personality, your relationships, etc. You are constantly preaching to yourself some kind of gospel. You preach to yourself an anti-gospel of your own righteousness, power, and wisdom, or you preach to yourself the true gospel of deep spiritual need and sufficient grace. You preach to yourself an anti-gospel of aloneness and inability, or you preach to yourself the true gospel of the presence, provisions, and the power of an ever-present Christ.[5]

Man, I wish a book like his with concepts like that had existed at the start of my gospel ministry. When I get to mentor students attending our local seminary, I make them read Tripp's book before any other resource. I want to give them a reality check about the dangers lying ahead. And I hope to spare them some of the mistakes I made, particularly when it comes to the pitfall of pride.

Gentleness

Sometimes the Bible refers to this same word as "meekness." Jesus declared in the Sermon on the Mount, "Blessed are the meek, for they shall inherit the earth" (Matt. 5:5). The word comes in two packages in the New Testament. First, it pertains to our relationship with God, where it reflects a disposition toward him that accepts without complaint everything that enters our lives. It consistently believes that Jesus works all things for the good of those who love him and are called according to his purpose (Rom. 8:28). It shows itself, for example, in the way we respond to his Word. "Therefore put away all filthiness and rampant wickedness and receive with meekness the implanted word, which is able to save your souls" (James 1:21).

Second, it pertains to our relationship with others. But please do not miss the connection between the two. Because by God's grace we keep our hearts soft, responsive, gentle, and meek before God, his Word, and his providences in our lives, that translates into a "strength-under-control" kind of gentleness with others, particularly when they may provoke us. The word was used in the culture to describe a wild horse that had been broken. This isn't weakness; it's meekness. It is what gave Jesus tremendous compassion with a woman caught in adultery in John 8:1–11 and yet tremendous strength in cleansing the temple of money-changers in John 2:13–17.

The importance of this peacemaking virtue stands out by the sheer amount of coverage it gets in the New Testament.

> But the fruit of the Spirit is love, joy, peace, patience, kindness, goodness, faithfulness, gentleness, [and] self-control. (Gal. 5:22–23)

> Brothers, if anyone is caught in any transgression, you who are spiritual should restore him in a spirit of gentleness. (Gal. 6:1)

44

And the Lord's servant must not be quarrelsome but kind to everyone, able to teach, patiently enduring evil, correcting his opponents with gentleness. (2 Tim. 2:24–25)

Remind them . . . to speak evil of no one, to avoid quarreling, to be gentle, and to show perfect courtesy toward all people. (Titus 3:1–2)

But in your hearts honor Christ the Lord as holy, always being prepared to make a defense to anyone who asks you for a reason for the hope that is in you; yet do it with gentleness and respect. (1 Pet. 3:15)

It really should matter to the captive and called of Jesus how we engage others. One might say a meek and gentle approach, especially in preserving peace in the body of Christ, is everything.

Patience

Paul uses a very interesting Greek word for this quality. He combines the words "long" and "suffering." So to be patient is to be long-suffering—to stay cool, calm, and collected even when provoked. You probably noticed it in the previous reference to the Fruit of the Spirit in Galatians 5:22. Paul lists both of these together in his letter to the Colossians: "Put on then, as God's chosen ones, holy and beloved, compassionate hearts, kindness, humility, meekness, and patience" (Col. 3:12). He targets preachers in particular regarding this virtue when he exhorts, "Preach the word, be ready in season and out of season; reprove, rebuke, and exhort, with complete patience and teaching" (2 Tim. 4:2). Complete patience. Sounds a lot like all humility! The first mark of love, Paul says, is that it is patient (1 Cor. 13:4). Patience relates very closely to the next virtue in Paul's list.

Forbearance

"[Bear] with one another in love" (Eph. 4:2). Humility, gentleness, and patience will combine in the heart of a peacemaker extraordinaire to endure a lot of others' sinfulness. These supernatural fruits will cause you to put up with a ton of nonsense. Paul commends the same again in Colossians: "[Bear] with one another and, if one has a complaint against another, [forgive] each other; as the Lord has forgiven you, so you also must forgive" (Col. 3:13). We forbear, Paul emphasizes, *in love*. And so he adds, "And above all these put on love, which binds everything together in perfect harmony" (v. 14). John Piper caught a twist on this that brings out the practical implications of what it looks like to forbear with others in the church:

> I am so glad Paul said we must endure one another. This frees me from the hypocritical need to think I, or anyone else in the church, am perfect. Perfect people don't need to be endured or forgiven. . . . But we do, often. Paul is not naïve. He knows that there are a few people at Bethlehem [substitute your own church] who are grumpy or critical or unreliable or finicky. He knows the pastor has gaping holes in the fabric of his sanctification. [No kidding, at least in my case.] So his counsel here is not how perfect people can live together in unity, but how real, imperfect Conference Baptists [substitute your own affiliation] can maintain the unity of the Spirit, namely, by *enduring* each other in love.[6]

One of our elders taught me a valuable practice for stressing the importance of patience and forbearance with newcomers to OGC. It actually occurred in the membership interview he conducted with Jan, my new bride (more on that story later), when she first came to our church. At one point Chuck asked her, "I've read your story in your membership application. I see that you tend to stay at a church for about four years. If you do decide to become a member at OGC, what makes you think you will stay at OGC for more than four years . . . and what will you do when we disappoint you?" Then, after a brief pause, he added, "Because we will disappoint you." Jan was surprised. She had thought for sure he would take the conversation in a different direction. But it made her stop and think about how the questions got to the heart of the matter. She replied, "I've been realizing that there is a pattern in my life of coming to a church and investing only to move on and do it again elsewhere. All I can say is that the Lord has brought me to a place where I am committed to put down roots somewhere for the long haul." About three years later I closed the deal on that commitment by making her the pastor's wife! But seriously, no one hangs in there with any church without cultivating the qualities of patience and forbearance—including the pastor and his wife.

Eagerness

Since chapter 1 made the case for this concluding virtue, there is no need to say much more. Excel at this. Do your best. Crave unity in the bond of peace in your church. If you do, then as Jesus's captive and called, you will take extraordinary pains with your approach to peacemaking shaped by grace. That takes humility, gentleness, patience, forbearance, and eagerness.

The Grace Approach

Here are some takeaways for fleshing out these virtues in safeguarding unity in the church.

First, set your sights first and foremost on pursuing a humble spirit in all your behavior toward God and others. No one summarizes this concept better than Edwards:

> Seek for a deep and abiding sense of your comparative meanness before God and man. Know God. Confess your nothingness and ill-desert before him. Distrust yourself. Rely on God. Renounce all glory except for him. Yield yourself heartily to his will and service. Avoid an aspiring, ambitious, ostentatious, assuming, arrogant, scornful, stubborn, willful, levelling, self-justifying behavior; and strive for more and more of the humble spirit that Christ manifested while he was on earth.[7]

Meditate often on Philippians 2:5–11 in striving for the humble spirit that is ours in Christ Jesus. Take extraordinary care in the way you talk to yourself—no other voice matters more than the one in your own head.

Second, if you find yourself needing to address an offense with someone, always carefully plan your approach in peacemaking. Think about the best time to engage. Never react from a place of high emotion, frustration, or defensiveness. Choose words carefully, knowing the power of the tongue (Prov. 18:21). Write out your appeal if necessary. Whenever you can, relate in person with someone as opposed to using the phone, social media, or email. Too much is lost in communication through those means. Writing about engaging difficult conversations, authors Stone, Patton, and Heen offer this advice:

> E-mail is a wildly efficient way to keep in touch. . . . For the day-to-day tasks of keeping up with a friend or moving a project forward, it's just about perfect.
>
> But ask e-mail to do anything even slightly more complicated in a relationship, and you can quickly run into trouble. . . . E-mail isn't dialogue—it's serial monologue. There's no opportunity to interrupt for clarification, to see the other's reaction and correct course, and to test our assumptions about their intentions before locking into interpretations and emotional reactions.
>
> E-mail doesn't convey tone of voice, facial expressions, or body language—all of which help us make sense of the sender's intentions.[8]

For these reasons and more I tell folks all the time—use email for information and affirmation, never confrontation.

Third, don't prematurely give up on pursuing reconciliation with others. Give your brothers and sisters time to process. Wait, wait, wait, wait. Just because you don't see a breakthrough on the first or second time doesn't mean that the Lord will not honor your efforts further down the road.

Fourth, when you think you've taken all you can take of the messiness others create in your life—and sometimes that can be true—more often than not, you can endure more. You can bear more. By God's grace and his Spirit's help, you can put up with more from the saints with which you share community in your church. If you give up too soon, you might end up bailing on the very means God has ordained for helping you grow in love and holiness. Church officers, adopt some version of the "What will you do when we disappoint you, because we will?" question in your vetting of candidates for membership in your church. Help folks see the absolute importance of these virtues to their longevity in your community.

Fifth, and most importantly, draw strength from the gospel to do all of the above. Soak in Colossians 3:13 regularly. "As the Lord has forgiven you"—put up with you, been patient with you, endured with you, been gentle with you, been humble toward you—"so you also must forgive."

It was said of Thomas Cranmer, sixteenth-century archbishop of the Church of England: "To do him any wrong was to beget a kindness from him."[9] It sounds to me like he was a peacemaker who radically shaped his approach with grace. How about you and me? Much of the answer to that question rides on the kind of theologians we are—the way we do or do not think about God.

4

Basing Our Thinking
as Peacemakers
on the Right Doctrine

Do not be conformed to this world, but be transformed by the renewal
of your mind.

Romans 12:2

Theology is unavoidable for every Christian. It is our attempt to understand the truth that God has revealed to us—something every Christian does. So it is not a question of whether we are going to engage in
theology; it is a question of whether our theology is sound or unsound.

R. C. Sproul[1]

A few years ago, I thought that my time at OGC was done. As my wife
and I packed for our annual fall trip to Idaho, a thought kept running
through my head: *It feels like I'm done—I'm 50 percent certain I'll
turn in my resignation letter when we get back.* I prayed in the quiet
of the wilderness for the Lord to speak clearly to me about so huge
a decision. That he did. He used two means during that vacation to
make me stay put—a verse of Scripture and a book. The verse? "And

say to Archippus, 'See that you fulfill the ministry that you have received in the Lord'" (Col. 4:17). That may not seem like much, but the moment I read it one morning, I heard the Spirit say (not audibly, but believe me, I got the message): *Tell Heffelfinger the same thing!* I'm grateful for many reasons that the Lord used his Word so powerfully that day, not the least of which is that I doubt I would be writing this if he hadn't.

The book? *Bad Religion: How We Became a Nation of Heretics*, by *New York Times* columnist Ross Douthat. He goes for the jugular early on in this no-holds-barred polemic:

> America's problem isn't too much religion, or too little of it. It's *bad* religion: the slow motion collapse of traditional Christianity and the rise of a variety of destructive pseudo-Christianities in its place. . . . The United States remains a deeply religious country, and most Americans are still drawing some water from the Christian well. But a growing number are inventing their own versions of what Christianity means, abandoning the nuances of traditional theology in favor of religions that stroke their egos and indulge or even celebrate their worst impulses. These faiths speak from many pulpits—conservative and liberal, political and pop-cultural, traditionally religious and fashionably "spiritual"—and many of their preachers call themselves Christian or claim a Christian warrant. But they are increasingly offering distortions of traditional Christianity, not the real thing.[2]

Both Douthat's critical analysis of the American religious landscape and his passionate plea for churches to return to a robust, confessional Christianity persuaded me to abandon any notions of stepping down. By God's grace, OGC's founders had linked us to just the kind of doctrinal substance Douthat advocates as part cure for our nation's spiritual ills.[3]

So why beat this doctrinal drum in a book about peacemaking that safeguards unity? The apostle Paul's model in Ephesians 4:4–6 inspires it. Once he brings into perspective our identity as captive and called peacemakers (v. 1) and then details a correct approach in relating as the same (vv. 2–3), his words turn decidedly theological in the next three verses. Paul shifts out of exhortation mode and launches into confession mode. As always with this apostle, the what-should-be of the Christian experience—in this case eagerly maintaining the unity of the Spirit in the bond of peace—flows from the what-actually-is of the Christian experience.

Motivation for becoming world-class peacemakers in the church requires doing sound theology in one biblical doctrine in particular: the Godhead. The argument goes something like this: if we think accurately about what Bible scholars call theology proper—the nature and character of God—then we will inevitably manifest a zeal for unity and a commitment to peacemaking. Tara Barthel and Judy Dabler, writing especially to women about peacemaking, stress this necessity of rigorous thinking about God in fostering right living for God:

> As we learn to walk through life firmly rooted in God's grace, living for his glory, we constantly *identify and evaluate* our thoughts and convictions in light of the truth of Scripture. Instead of only addressing our behavior, we ask, "What are the deeply held beliefs that influence my emotions, thoughts, and actions?" and "How do my beliefs line up with Scripture?" We then reject any beliefs that are false, affirm those that are true, and take practical steps to live out our faith in loving Christian community.[4]

Pastors, teachers, small group leaders, disciple-making believers investing in others—how committed are we to imparting sound doctrine at the heart of our ministries? Do you stress the whole counsel of God (Acts 20:27) in your teaching, including even demanding doctrinal sections, or do you cherry pick texts to suit your own agenda? I remember a season in the heyday of the church growth movement where I slipped into a dangerous pattern. Wanting the church to grow by attracting new people, I started favoring more prescriptive, practical, how-to, application passages of Scripture to the neglect of the more indicative, theological, what-is portions. In the process I risked robbing my people of the thought-shaping biblical underpinnings they needed for rightly influencing their choices in everyday life.

Pastor A. W. Tozer wrote powerful devotional literature in his day. Words like these from his books have challenged my approach to teaching that ensures a comprehensive approach to Scripture—especially regarding who God is and what he is like:

> What comes into our minds when we think about God is the most important thing about us. The history of mankind will probably show that

no people has ever risen above its religion, and man's spiritual history will positively demonstrate that no religion has ever been greater than its idea of God. Worship is pure or base as the worshiper entertains high or low thoughts of God.

For this reason the gravest question before the Church is always God himself, and the most portentous fact about any man is not what he at a given time may say or do, but what he in his deep heart conceives God to be like. We tend by a secret law of the soul to move toward our mental image of God. This is true not only of the individual Christian, but of the company of Christians that composes the Church. Always the most revealing thing about the Church is her idea of God.[5]

If Tozer is right—and I'm convinced he is—then nothing matters more in church teaching ministries than imparting truth that helps people think correctly about God so they can live rightly before him. Paul does precisely that as he turns his thoughts to the relationship between an eagerness to preserve unity and our knowledge of God.

Ones Everywhere

In his campaign to make us eager preservers of unity, Paul works hard to equip us with some deeply held beliefs about God. It is difficult to miss the main thrust in verses 4–6, isn't it? Seven different times we read the word *one*. We have "one body," "one Spirit," "one hope," "one Lord," "one faith," "one baptism," and "one God and Father." Do you think the man is trying to tell us something? Belief #1—God is into oneness. Another emphasis doesn't jump off the page quite so readily, but observe closely and you'll see it: God's oneness somehow involves a "threeness." Enter the mystery of the Trinity![6] Paul's confession of faith regarding the Godhead references all three persons of our triune God: the Holy Spirit (v. 4), the Lord—God's Son (v. 5), and God the Father (v. 6). Belief #2—God's oneness manifests itself in a perfect unity of diverse persons.

Dr. Martyn Lloyd-Jones distilled this essential takeaway belief with remarkable economy of words:

The unity of the Church is a manifestation of the perfection of the Godhead. . . . We should see ourselves as members of the Church, and see the Church as a reflection on earth of the oneness of the Triune God—Three in One, One in Three, Holy Spirit, Son, Father.[7]

Dr. Edmund Clowney powerfully connects the dots between Paul's exhortation for eager preserving of unity with the doctrinal truth of God's oneness:

> The term that Paul uses here is stronger than is suggested by the translation "make every effort." It actually means our total dedication to the unity of God himself. We are to be one because we serve one God. If we served many gods—Isis, Apollo, Dionysos, Demeter—then we might form different cults, for there were "gods many and lords many." But we serve the one true God, who is also the heavenly Father of his one family (Eph. 3:14).[8]

There Is One Body

Six out of seven of Paul's *ones* pertain directly to the doctrine of God. The first in the list, however, does not. "There is one body" (Eph. 4:4). With this he hopes to instill in us another deeply held, unity-promoting theological belief concerning the doctrine of the church. He will hit theology proper hard, for sure, but not before addressing ecclesiology: the nature, function, and mission of the church.

Throughout his epistles Paul used multiple word pictures to describe the church. But the church as a body may well have been his favorite. The best-known passage of the kind elsewhere in the New Testament reads: "For as in one body we have many members, and the members do not all have the same function, so we, though many, are one body in Christ, and individually members one of another" (Rom. 12:4–5). Paul also used the image earlier in Ephesians 2:16 to explain how God reconciles Jew and Gentile "in one body through the cross." And he returned to it again in Ephesians 4:16, 4:23, and 5:30. What a vivid illustration! There is one body; it consists of diverse members. Belief #3—this is unity, not uniformity. The picture calls for harmony, not conformity. We can credit Barthel and Dabler for this distinction based on Paul's doctrinal instruction:

> Even in our differences we can have unity, because unity is a lot like "harmony." Harmony involves the playing of different musical notes or chords

which, even when performed together, create a pleasing and beautiful blend. Harmony is music where varying notes are unified under a set of principles. For us to have unity in the body of Christ, we have been called to be unified in our submission to the headship of Christ. In order to maintain charitable hearts toward one another, we are to remember that our unity comes from an understanding of the foundation of our unity: "There is one body."[9]

One way our church has sought to apply this "one body" emphasis from its inception surrounds the issue of baptism. Let me warn you upfront before you read further: this may rile you. I admit we take a minority position among credo-baptists who immerse only professing believers. Now, we don't teach anything but believer's baptism. We don't practice paedo-baptism—the sprinkling of infants. In fact, when I teach our new member candidates on the subject, I don't tell those who have been baptized as infants that they need to be rebaptized; I tell them they need to really be *baptized*.

Okay? That's where I've landed on the position. But I'm savvy enough to know that nothing I will ever teach or write on this subject will ultimately turn the tide of differing opinions on this controversial and potentially divisive matter. Good grief; far more intelligent scholars than I have articulated the opposite position. I once heard Dr. Sinclair Ferguson, teaching a doctoral level ecclesiology class, make his case for paedo-baptism. It nearly resulted in an Agrippa-like, "In a short time you will persuade me to be a Presbyterian" statement on my part. Believe me, when I get to heaven, I plan to report ASAP to Room 201— *The Truth about Baptism*—right after I get finished down the hall in Room 101—*The Truth about the Millennium*. You might not care for where I've landed on that one either. Ah, yes, so many opportunities to practice unity characterized by harmony vs. uniformity!

Now that I've exhausted every disclaimer I can muster about our conciliatory approach to baptism, here is how our bylaws read:

As our confession states, we teach and practice believer's baptism by immersion. However, we realize that among some Reformed traditions the meaning and mode of baptism is controversial. We flatly deny the aberrant views of baptismal regeneration. We would humbly encourage anyone with a different view of baptism to investigate the scriptural evidence for believer's baptism. Having made this statement, we acknowledge that many Bible-believing Christians who show every evidence of saving grace in their lives are convinced that infant baptism is a sign and seal of the covenant of grace that can be validly inferred from scripture. For them it is a matter of conscience, even as believer's baptism is for us. We would warn anyone against refusing to be immersed as a believer due to ignorance or pride. If however, it is a matter of conviction, we will not ask them to violate their conscience in order to be received as members with full privileges. We will commit ourselves to unity in the faith of our Lord Jesus Christ and allow each person to be fully convinced in his or her own mind. Those who do not hold to believer's baptism will not be permitted to vote on any amendments bearing on that issue.[10]

Before you send me an email or write me a letter about this, take a deep breath. You don't have to agree with our position and practice. I simply offer it as one example of how our thinking about God dictates our practice in a difficult matter. You can think of a number of others, I am sure. Are your approach, policy, and practice at least tempered as a board, as a committee, as a team, and as a church on the whole by a "there is one body" sentiment in the mix? Paul would say it must.

One Spirit Who Calls

The apostle doesn't linger long on the doctrine of the church in his argument, but those four little words—"there is one body"—contain a ton of peacemaking motivation. He focuses the rest of the way on the doctrine of God. It's worth noting that all these "ones" from Paul's stylus come first in the Greek sentence structure for emphasis. He works overtime to drill into us the importance of oneness in God and the passion for peace it should generate in the church. He starts with the Spirit, the Third Person of the Trinity, because he left off there at the end of verse 3. The Spirit gifts the church its unity in the bond of peace. A particular work of the Spirit now warrants mentioning with the words, "just as you were called to the one hope that belongs to your call" (Eph. 4:4).

That concept of calling should sound familiar. Remember where we started? "Walk in a manner worthy of the calling to which you have been called" (v. 1). The Spirit of God powerfully works in the life of every elect person to call them out of darkness into light (1 Pet. 2:9), giving them one hope. Paul had prayed already about this for them:

"Having the eyes of your hearts enlightened, that you may know what is the hope to which he has called you" (Eph. 1:18). Peter refers to it as "a living hope" in 1 Peter 1:3–4:

> Blessed be the God and Father of our Lord Jesus Christ! According to his great mercy, he has caused us to be born again to a living hope through the resurrection of Jesus Christ from the dead, to an inheritance that is imperishable, undefiled, and unfading, kept in heaven for you.

By the effective work of the Spirit in calling us and causing us to be born again (John 3:3, 5), we now all enjoy the same hope—a certain expectation of the imaginably rich inheritance of heaven that awaits us and is being kept for us until we go home to our reward. That singular hope should galvanize us as peacemakers.

I remember one occasion in particular where the Spirit's calling and my hope of heaven compelled important peacemaking choices on my part.

While on sabbatical in 2014, I met with the man who had led me to Jesus over forty years ago. To this day I remain tremendously thankful for the way God used Don in my conversion experience. Unfortunately, our relationship had deteriorated over time due to some difficult interpersonal dynamics in his leadership style. We eventually parted ways. Thirty years had passed since we last fellowshipped together. The Lord had helped me release any resentment toward him for quite some time. But we had never addressed the past offenses—wrongs quite honestly too severe for me to overlook (Prov. 19:11). Some peacemaking types from our past had recently managed to reconnect us. Eventually I chose to write him—something I wished I had done long before, and a failure I needed to confess—expressing my concern that so much in our history remained unresolved. If he wished, I would take some free time to meet with him while in the Boston area.

He agreed. I didn't know what to expect. Honestly, being the conflict avoider I am, I really hoped he would decline. But anything less than an all-in commitment on my part would have fallen short of the standard Paul calls for in Ephesians 4. We spent three hours together one Saturday in a coffee shop. He brought my letter with him. We plowed through each and every issue—line by line. When we finished, he looked at me and said, "Curt, I didn't realize what I was doing at the time. I see now how much I hurt you." And then he asked my forgiveness for it all. In the end we embraced and went away reconciled. God was pleased. We both excelled that day, by God's grace, as peacemakers.

One of the main motivations compelling me to engage in that painful process came right from Paul's words about the Spirit's calling. Like me, Don is a believer. He has the same hope of heaven I do. I will see him there. We will worship the Lamb around the throne together. We will do business in the New Heavens and New Earth together. Far better, if possible, to be reconciled on this side of things, because we know for certain we will on the other side. I am so grateful God allowed us to mend the fence sooner rather than later. And we continue to connect from time to time by phone and mail as the Lord leads.

One Lord Who Saves

"One Lord" (Eph. 4:5). The Old Testament only ever uses the word "LORD" to refer to Yahweh, the God of Israel—the One spoken of in the Hebrew Shema ("hear") this way: "Hear, O Israel: The LORD our God, the LORD is one" (Deut. 6:4). In Ephesians 4:5 Paul equates the Son of God, Jesus, with God, calling him "Lord." This reference joins numerous others that testify to the deity of Jesus. The apostle does the very same thing in a letter to the Corinthians: "Yet for us there is one God, the Father, from whom are all things and for whom we exist, and one Lord, Jesus Christ, through whom are all things and through whom we exist" (1 Cor. 8:6).

Just as there is one Spirit who calls, Paul adds the work of the one Lord Jesus: he is the One who saves. The terms "one faith" and "one baptism" combine to capture the same Christological truth. They both point to Jesus's saving work as the Mediator who bore the penalty for our sins on the cross and imputes his 100 percent righteousness to us by faith (2 Cor. 5:21). Paul uses "faith" as in "the faith"—the essential gospel doctrines that summarize Christianity. Jude 3 does the same thing: "I found it necessary to write appealing to you to contend for *the faith* that was once for all delivered to the saints" (emphasis added).

Few ministries in this generation have served the church better in terms of articulating "the faith" with utmost clarity and biblical fidelity than 9Marks:

> This Gospel, then, is that God is our holy Creator and righteous Judge. He created us to glorify him and enjoy him forever, but we have all sinned, both in Adam as our representative head, and in our own individual actions (Rom. 5:12; 3:23). We therefore deserve death—spiritual separation from God in hell (Rom. 6:23; Eph. 2:3)—and are in fact already spiritually stillborn, helpless in our sins (Ps. 51:5; Rom. 5:6–8; Eph. 2:1) and in need of God to impart spiritual life to us (Ezek. 37:1–14; John 3:3). But God sent his Son Jesus Christ, fully God and fully man (Phil. 2:5–11), to die the death that we deserved, and He raised Him up for our justification, proving that He was God's Son (Rom. 5:1; 1:4). If we would have Christ's perfect righteousness credited to us, and the penalty for our sins accounted to him, we must repent of our sins and believe in Jesus Christ for salvation (2 Cor. 5:21; Mark 1:14–15).[11]

But what about the term "one baptism"? Does he mean Spirit baptism (1 Cor. 12:13), or does he have in mind water baptism (Rom. 6:3–4)? There are cogent arguments for both. Here's why I lean to the latter, given the context. Paul appeals to the saving work of Jesus based upon the truths of "the faith." Baptism, regardless of mode—though immersion in my humble, peacemaking baptistic opinion best illustrates the truth—represents identification with Jesus's saving work through his death, burial, and resurrection. He commands all who believe to follow him in baptism (Matt. 28:19). This ordinance is the one and only initiation rite for us that points to our unity in Christ and our incorporation into his one body.

One Father Who Reigns

"One God and Father of all, who is over all and through all and in all" (Eph. 4:6). What a finish! Once again, please don't forget the context here. This concerns the church. While it is true that God reigns and rules over all creation, that is not the primary emphasis in this passage. Paul writes about the body of Christ. And along with his seven "ones," he brings this theological treatise to a climax with four "alls"—"Father of all," "over all," "through all," and "in all." This applies to Jew and Gentile alike. God is Father of every ethnicity, every background, every nationality, every people, every tribe, and every tongue.

Put these truths all together, and what do we behold with awe? There is one God and Father who reigns over all as sovereign King. There is one God and Father who blesses all through the mediatorial work of Jesus, the Lord. And there is one God and Father who dwells in all by his Spirit. When all this theology grips us as our own treasured, deeply held beliefs, eagerness might not even begin to describe our passion for preserving unity in the church.

So, the big takeaway question from this chapter is this: How much of a God-centered, biblical thinker are you? The answer matters greatly in determining how much or how little you will excel as a peacemaker determined to safeguard the unity of the Spirit in the bond of peace. The Great Commandment (Matt. 22:36–39) tells us to love God, among other things, with "all our mind." We are to be vigorous thinkers about God and his church. The more we dwell on God—Father, Son, and Spirit as one—and the church—one body with many members—the more stoked the fires of our love will be for others in maintaining unity in the body. Thomas Goodwin (1600–1679), one of the English Puritan pastors, observed this circular relationship between thoughts about God and affections for him leading to more thinking about him and doing for him:

> Indeed, thoughts and affections are . . . the mutual cause of each other: "Whilst I mused, the fire burned" (Ps. 39:3); so that thoughts are the bellows that kindle and inflame affections; and if they are inflamed, they cause new thoughts to boil.[12]

I trust our journey through Ephesians 4:1–6 has helped you embrace more enthusiastically than ever the biblical priorities essential to preserving unity in Jesus's church: seeing yourself as a peacemaker in the right light—captive and called—shaping your approach as a peacemaker with the right touch—redolent with grace—and basing your thinking as a peacemaker on the right doctrine—one body and one God. This is Priority One of a worthy walk in Jesus.

Before we head off to part 2, let's take a few moments to ponder some important questions from our study.

First, where in the scheme of your concerns as a follower of Jesus does peacemaking fall? Does it come anywhere close to the ranking Paul gives it in these verses? Which of the three priorities needs the most attention? What practical steps can you take in that one area to ratchet up your preserving unity quotient in your church? With whom might you share these goals to enlist some gospel accountability for your progress in this strategic area?

Second, with whom are you at odds, if anyone? Hang on now. Give this some time. You might even want to pray a prayer like David's: "Search me, O God, and know my heart! Try me and know my thoughts! And see if there be any grievous way in me, and lead me in the way everlasting" (Ps. 139:23–24)! Where have things broken down in one of your relationships, no matter how insignificant? Have you done all you possibly can do on your end of things to promote reconciliation (Rom. 12:18)? The people at Peacemaker Ministries are fond of saying, "You may only be 2 percent responsible for a conflict, but you're 100 percent responsible for your 2 percent." What else might Jesus lead you to do to help move the logjam?

Third, how much do you know about the nature and character of God? How much attention have you given to cultivating biblically sound and deeply held beliefs in this peacemaking-critical sphere of theology? What resource could you study to increase your knowledge of his glorious Triune Person? Consider investing in a solid one-volume systematic theology like the ones referenced in this chapter. That just might make good sense for beefing up your doctrinal mastery in this area. You could even get über-intentional, like a dear friend of mine did in a recent email:

> Hey Curt, I have a request to make and I realize that it is sizable, so please feel free to answer how you see fit. The ask is this: I have been realizing the stagnation and lack of discipline in my life and my walk with the Lord and I would like to deal with that and move forward. I realize to do that I need some outside direction and counsel from someone who understands such things. So, I am asking if you would be willing to be a "spiritual director" for me for some period of time. What I am thinking is if we could meet for one hour every other week for a couple months and then reevaluate and adjust from there (less frequent, not at all, keep the same, etc.). I realize you are busy with many things. I would be delighted to compensate

you for your time if that would be helpful to you (it might also be helpful to me to have more "skin in the game"). In any case, regardless of your answer, know that I consider you a good, kind, and faithful friend.

My friend's request didn't pertain to a peacemaking issue *per se*, but it serves as an excellent example of someone taking initiative to secure a 2 Timothy 2:2 discipleship relationship to help advance his spiritual growth. Do you have someone like that in your life? Peacemaking effectiveness is only one benefit to potentially increase as a result from such intentionality in your walk with God.

Finally, where must you confess an absence of the virtues of grace-shaped peacemaking in some relationship—humility, gentleness, patience, forbearance, and eagerness? Will you bring those failures even now to the cross and confess them to the Lord (1 John 1:9)? Believe Jesus and his gospel once again for his forgiving grace. Trust him all over again to help you obey him in excelling still more in love for your brothers and sisters (1 Thess. 4:9–10).

Thomas Watson connected the dots between our doctrine and practice as peacemakers eager to safeguard the unity of our churches:

> There is but one God, and they that serve him should be one. There is nothing that would render the true religion more lovely, or make more proselytes to it, than to see the professors of it tied together with the heart-strings of love. Behold how good and how pleasant a thing it is, to see brethren live together in unity! If God be one, let all that profess him be of one mind, and one heart, and thus fulfil Christ's prayer, "that they all may be one."[13]

If only it were that simple and easy! Deidra Riggs summarized the problem succinctly: "Despite our good intentions, passion for justice, or desire to 'defend the gospel,' we often let ourselves get in the way."[14] Indeed we do. More than one obstacle can block our success in embracing the biblical priorities for eagerly preserving unity in the church. God's Word contains just the counsel we need to keep ourselves out of the way in fighting the good fight for the unity of the Spirit in the bond of peace.

PART TWO

Avoiding the Pitfalls That Threaten Unity in Jesus's Church

5

Murdering

Staying out of "Prison"—the How of Settling Disputes

Know this, my beloved brothers: let every person be quick to hear, slow to speak, slow to anger; for the anger of man does not produce the righteousness of God.

James 1:19–20

Conflict has an uncanny ability to make the best of theologians and saints live like brute beasts.

Alfred Poirier[1]

Our church made a terrific hire not too long ago. We brought on staff an associate pastor of administration. This pastor, Mike, relatively young but mature beyond his years and with a genius intellect, startled me one day with an observation. "Curt, the thing that has surprised me the most since entering full-time ministry is the amount of anger I've observed among Christians." He clearly did not mean the Ephesians 4:26, "be angry and do not sin" version. At his tender age he had already seen more than enough of the James 1:20, "does not produce the righteousness of God" variety. If there is any pitfall that continually threatens unity in Jesus's church, look no further than this one. Alexander Strauch concurs:

One of the most important biblical principles for handling conflict constructively is to control the passions of anger. Most disputes wouldn't be nearly as unpleasant and unprofitable if people didn't lose control of their tempers and say harsh and irrational things to one another. Unrestrained anger creates and escalates conflict. It makes problem solving and peacemaking far more difficult than it should be. It is how we most viciously bite and devour one another (Gal. 5:15).[2]

Any hope of doing our best at preserving unity in Jesus's church demands we slay the giant of wrath, which lurks in all our hearts. Jesus wasted no time in taking it on early in his teaching in the Sermon on the Mount. In doing so he showed how a peacemaker's ethic has everything to do with avoiding its trap. Before we camp out on this liberating truth, consider this insight about God's law, the context of Jesus's teaching about anger:

> John Newton, the converted slave trader and author of the hymn "Amazing Grace," was also an outstandingly wise correspondent with many of his contemporaries who sought his spiritual counsel. In one of his letters he wrote, "Ignorance of the nature and design of the law is at the bottom of most of our religious mistakes." That is still true today. Perhaps more Christians are confused or uncertain about the role that God's law plays in their lives than about most things.[3]

That was certainly the case in Jesus's day. A plain reading of Matthew 5:21–48 settles it. A total of six times in that treatment of the Law, Jesus presented what Bible interpreters refer to as "antitheses" in the form of "You have heard that it was said" followed by "But I say to you." In the prior context he had already declared himself the very fulfillment of the Old Testament law of God (Matt. 5:17). He also demanded of his followers a standard of righteousness that exceeded Israel's religious elite of the day (v. 20). Failure to manifest a lifestyle of righteousness beyond that of the scribes and Pharisees, he warned, would result in catastrophic, eternal consequences—"you will never enter the kingdom of heaven" (v. 20). All of that set the stage for the Lord to then establish himself as the foremost and most authoritative interpreter of the Law in the rest of the chapter.

He leads off with the sixth commandment—"You shall not murder" (Exod. 20:13; Deut. 5:17).

You have heard that it was said to those of old, "You shall not murder; and whoever murders will be liable to judgment." But I say to you that everyone who is angry with his brother will be liable to judgment; whoever insults his brother will be liable to the council; and whoever says, "You fool!" will be liable to the hell of fire. So if you are offering your gift at the altar and there remember that your brother has something against you, leave your gift there before the altar and go. First be reconciled to your brother, and then come and offer your gift. Come to terms quickly with your accuser while you are going with him to court, lest your accuser hand you over to the judge, and the judge to the guard, and you be put in prison. Truly, I say to you, you will never get out until you have paid the last penny. (Matt. 5:21–26)

Avoiding anger's pitfall requires that we get Jesus's big idea on the subject: "Do your best" peacemakers receive the deeper/broader implications of the sixth commandment. I chose the verb *receive* with care. I borrowed it from the epistles. "Therefore put away all filthiness and rampant wickedness and receive with meekness the implanted word, which is able to save your souls" (James 1:21). So much hinges on how we respond to Jesus's teaching here—indeed, to the Scriptures as a whole. The goal always remains the same in putting ourselves under the teaching of God's Word. We are to take in what is taught with a humble, softhearted receptivity. I often pray this verse before I preach a message on Sunday mornings. I ask the Lord that his truth might take root deep within us, such that it transforms the very way we live our lives.

We promote this kind of humble receptivity to God's Word in our newcomer class as well. When we cover our core value of expository preaching—verse-by-verse treatment of whole books of the Bible—I offer our folks as a gift Christopher Ash's helpful booklet, *Listen Up! A Practical Guide to Listening to Sermons.* Churches desiring excellence in peacemaking would do well to stock it for their people in their resource centers. Commenting on James 1:21, Ash writes:

> It is very hard to get me to understand and accept the teaching of the Bible when my comfort, my lifestyle, my complacency, and my selfishness all depend on my not understanding and accepting it.
>
> To listen humbly is to be realistic about this. What is more, it is to recognise that there is more than one way to evade the challenge of the Bible. . . . The more common way . . . is to find a clever way to reinterpret

the Bible so I can persuade myself that, although I must admit it looks as if it challenges me, in fact it doesn't. This preserves my impression of piety while safeguarding my rebellion against God. . . . To listen humbly is to admit that the Bible is right and I am wrong, that God is God and I need to change.[4]

The subtleties of anger, perhaps more than many other challenging themes, may more readily activate our inner defense lawyers when confronted with God's Word on the subject.[5] Jesus outlines two crucial implications to a deeper/wider/broader, more-than-skin deep understanding of the sixth commandment in Matthew 5. The problem with the scribes and Pharisees, with whom Jesus sparred frequently, was not that they missed the boat in interpreting "You shall not murder." They understood it made one liable to judgment, justice in the courts, and even the death penalty (Num. 35:31). Why? God created humanity in his own image (Gen. 9:6). Murder assaults God, whom he designed us to image. No, their error lay with limiting the commandment's intent to that alone. In the rest of these verses, Jesus set the record straight.

Avoid Unrighteous Anger at All Costs

"Everyone who is angry with his brother will be liable to judgment" (v. 22). Some manuscripts add the phrase "without cause" to the text. "Everyone who is angry with his brother *without cause* will be liable to judgment" (emphasis added). Most regard that as a later addition not in the original manuscripts. But no doubt it captures a proper interpretation of the text. Jesus doesn't dismiss righteous indignation, as we like to call it, in his teaching here. He demonstrated it himself with a much-needed temple cleansing later in Matthew 21:12–13.

No, the Lord takes aim here at the opposite. He has unrighteous anger—the kind rooted in pride, selfishness, bitterness, hatred, malice, and revenge—in his sights. He drills down beneath the behavioral and external obvious application of the sixth commandment to its ultimate source: hatred in the heart and the anger it generates. He wants us to get this at all costs. To give way to unrighteous anger in the heart makes us subject to God's judgment as much as actual homicide. It's murder alright—just without weapons.

Consider some other texts that warn about the sin of anger and its devastating consequences:

> A man of wrath stirs up strife,
>> and one given to anger causes much transgression. (Prov. 29:22)

Now the works of the flesh are evident: sexual immorality, impurity, sensuality, idolatry, sorcery, enmity, strife, jealousy, *fits of anger*, rivalries, dissensions, divisions, envy, drunkenness, orgies, and things like these. I warn you, as I warned you before, that those who do such things will not inherit the kingdom of God. (Gal. 5:19–21, emphasis added)

Let all bitterness and wrath and anger and clamor and slander be put away from you, along with all malice. (Eph. 4:31)

Know this, my beloved brothers: let every person be quick to hear, slow to speak, slow to anger; for the anger of man does not produce the righteousness of God. (James 1:19–20)

Everyone who hates his brother is a murderer, and you know that no murderer has eternal life abiding in him. (1 John 3:15)

Murder's Weapon of Choice

God certainly means business with so many warnings aimed at the sin of unbridled anger. And though I called it "murder without weapons" earlier, that's not entirely accurate. Anger has a particularly potent weapon of choice for killing. It's called the tongue. Taking no prisoners, Jesus lays on the conviction even heavier in our text. "Whoever *insults* his brother will be liable to the council; and whoever *says*, 'You fool!' will be liable to the hell of fire" (Matt. 5:22, emphasis added). The Greek word for "insults" was a quasi-expletive of the day. If you really wanted to lay a put-down on somebody back then, that word would do it. It meant something like "stupid," "knucklehead," or "idiot." The second slur, "fool," got even uglier. It slammed a person's morals. Think "pervert," "scoundrel," or "reprobate." I wonder if Jesus might have had this Old Testament reference in the back of his mind at

71

that moment: "There is one whose rash words are like sword thrusts" (Prov. 12:18).

Can we wrap our minds around this? What comes out of our mouths is the best barometer of the condition of our hearts. "The good person out of the good treasure of his heart produces good, and the evil person out of his evil treasure produces evil, for out of the abundance of the heart his mouth speaks" (Luke 6:45). We are warned strenuously about this elsewhere:

> No human being can tame the tongue. It is a restless evil, full of deadly poison. With it we bless our Lord and Father, and with it we curse people who are made in the likeness of God. From the same mouth come blessing and cursing. My brothers, these things ought not to be so. (James 3:8–10)

No wonder Jesus goes so far to say these words later in the Gospel of Matthew: "I tell you, on the day of judgment people will give account for every careless word they speak" (12:36). A believing friend of mine once shared with me a deep wound inflicted by sharp words. An email exchange over a church conflict referred to him as "a festering pus." I could hardly believe the words as I read them on the page. It never ceases to amaze me how unchecked anger can lead to careless words that cut to the core of a person's being.

That same judgment theme, including ultimately the horrors of eternal condemnation in hell, permeates this teaching in the Sermon on the Mount. Three different synonyms relating to the consequences of unchecked anger of the heart and the abusive words it spews forth appear in the text. The first two, "judgment" and "the council," refer to the Sanhedrin, Israel's Supreme Court, and the third is "hell of fire." Jesus doesn't mean to convey increasing degrees of seriousness with each of these; he wants to get across that unrighteous anger is far more serious than we often dare think. If we don't repent, grave consequences await. We will never enter the kingdom of heaven. Rageaholics beware!

The Lord has a way of getting our attention about the sin in our lives. I'll never forget the circumstances in which he first busted me about my problem with anger. During our two sons' middle school days, our family sought help from a Christian counselor. The Heff household suffered from a serious lack of peace. One session, the counselor sat us on the floor in a circle. She asked each of us to write down an animal that best described each of the other members of the family. When she came to Josh, his choice for me? Bear—a grizzly. Joel? Same thing. Grizzly bear. Both chose the very same thing without looking at the other's answer. Mind you, not teddy, koala, brown, or cuddly bear—but big, bad, ugly, angry grizzly bear. Talk about leveled to the ground by God's Spirit! I got the point. It was time to declare war on my anger.

Hi, I'm Curt and I'm a Rageaholic

This sin problem in particular so frequently plagues our churches it requires a serious battle plan for defeating it. I don't pretend to know everything on the subject, by any stretch of the imagination. However, I have fought and continue to fight with anger. From my experience and truth of the Scripture, let me suggest some strategies for doing exactly what the Bible commands us to do: "Put to death therefore what is earthly in you. . . . But now you must put them all away: anger, wrath, malice, slander, and obscene talk from your mouth" (Col. 3:5, 8). This is the "mortification of sin," as Puritan John Owen dubbed it so long ago.[6]

1. Own It

Let's face it. We all do it. Instead of admitting our bankruptcy of spirit (Matt. 5:5) and mourning over our sin (v. 6), we tend to minimize it. We rationalize it. We can even deny it. "Hey, I don't have a problem with anger; I'm just honest!" Like the recovery folks like to say, "Denial's not just a river in Egypt." Worse than all of the above, we can get defensive. No question about it. "The struggle to accept our exceeding sinfulness is everywhere in the church of Christ. We accept the doctrine of total depravity, but when we are approached about our own sin, we wrap our robes of self-righteousness around us and rise to our own defense."[7]

May I make a suggestion? Pray a prayer like David's: "Search me, O God, and know my heart! Try me and know my thoughts! And see if there be any grievous way in me, and lead me in the way everlasting" (Ps. 139:23–24)! Pray it often. How about asking your spouse, kids, roommate, best friend, pastor—anyone you know who loves you and genuinely looks out for your interests—to imagine the animal which best describes you? Or, if you want to try an even bolder approach, just flat-out ask that person, "Where, possibly, do you see any pattern of anger in my life?" But take care; if you want to get this step right, please see the next strategy.

2. Recognize It

I say "rageaholic" and you think what? Temper tantrum. We envisage someone melting down with explosive emotion. True enough. But, unfortunately, anger puts on a number of other far more subtle and insidious faces in our lives. Doctors Carter and Minirth clarified this dynamic for me:

> When most people think of anger, they picture a person in rage. They have images of slamming doors, shouting, and intimidating communication. Certainly this is *part* of the angry response. But anger is not that one-dimensional. It is multi-faceted; therefore it should not be stereotyped. It can be found in any temperament. Whether a person is shy or extroverted, perfectionistic or laid-back, he or she can show anger in many ways. We use the term *anger* to describe a number of expressions: frustrations, irritability, annoyance, blowing off steam, fretting. It is important to realize how each of these reactions is tied to anger.[8]

Allow me to share my preferred anger-face of choice. Sad to say, I mastered this relational strategy over decades of marriage. Blow up, yell and scream, lose control? Me? No way. Men of God don't act that way. Not a chance. But what about withdrawal, cold shoulder, passive-aggressive, shutdown tactics? When I'm mad, I can even navigate our relatively small kitchen by avoiding the slightest touch with my bride. She gets the mega-silent treatment from her Mr. Spiritual Husband. And I can still struggle with this ugliness after all these years, I must admit.

3. Suspect It

Robert D. Jones, in his excellent treatment of what he calls the common problem of anger, goes so far as to contend that "nearly all human anger is sinful."[9] It doesn't take much for our deceitful, desperately sick hearts (Jer. 17:9) to start sliding down the slippery slope from so-called righteous indignation into sinful anger. That's why James warns, "Let every person be quick to hear, slow to speak, slow to anger, for the anger of man does not produce the righteousness of God" (James 1:19–20). A default healthy suspicion of the likely nature of passions within us—the cause of quarrels and fights within our churches (4:1)—will go a long way toward keeping us in this safe zone: "A fool gives full vent to his spirit, but a wise man quietly holds it back" (Prov. 29:11).

4. Tag-Team It

Don't wage this war alone. Capitalize on the wisdom of old. "Iron sharpens iron, and one man sharpens another" (27:17). Just about the same time I came to grips with some of my issues in this area, a member of my church came to me about some troubles in his marriage. The more we dug into the situation, the clearer it became that both of us struggled in quite similar ways with anger. With a "two are better than one" (Eccles. 4:9) hopefulness galvanizing our souls, we set out to fight the good fight together.

For six months, my friend and I met for breakfast at a local restaurant just about every Saturday morning. We worked our way a chapter at a time through *The Anger Workbook*. The genius of this resource lies in its workbook format. In addition to engaging the helpful content, the reader navigates a thirteen-step interactive plan to process the concepts. Having someone else to act as an accountability partner and sympathetic sounding board along the journey also proved immensely helpful. We both resonated with this conclusion toward the end of the workbook: "when you confess your anger to a trusted friend, two things can occur. First, you are able to find help and support from someone who loves you, and second, you feel more accountable to follow through with your plans to be emotionally appropriate in the future."[10]

5. Examine It

Our church's attorney, David, also happens to be a certified Christian conciliator. He has done a lot of conflict coaching and mediation in that role. David favors a particular word picture to describe getting beyond opponents' conflicting viewpoints. He aims to expose their motives/ interests beneath the surface, and he calls this "scuba diving" in the heart. He wants to get at the heart idols beneath the sins contributing to the dispute. It involves the skillful use of questions designed to draw out the heart to that end (Prov. 20:5).[11]

In our war on rage, we need to do the very same thing ourselves. We need to dive down beneath the surface of our angry responses to ask ourselves why we react the way we do. Sometimes this reveals a level of brokenness in our lives even more insidious than the anger itself. If we don't repent on that deeper level, we might never break free of its grip upon us.

At the end of 2014, Nancy, the wife of my youth, was diagnosed with stage three ovarian cancer. They call that form of the stupid disease "the silent killer," because many women don't experience symptoms until it is too late. Nancy's diagnosis was serious, but her odds for a cure were promising. On most issues throughout our married lives, we enjoyed uncommon oneness. We typically got quickly on the same page on major decisions affecting our household. Not so in this case. We clashed over the course of treatment she would pursue to save her life. We simply didn't agree.

Wouldn't you know it? When I didn't get my way, I went into sulk mode. I shut her out—way out. It got so bad one night she confronted me just before we turned out the lights. "I feel like you've already buried me," she said. Leveled again. Time to repent once more.

But this time around the Lord helped me do some self-critique like I hadn't before. I wrestled with the "why" question behind my response to her. He revealed my root issue—fear of another loss. Our eldest son had died of heart failure at only thirty-five years of age just a few years before. Even the thought of the same thing happening to my wife terri-fied me, and I set out to control her choices by punishing her through emotional withdrawal. I experienced what the authors describe in *How People Change*:

> You begin to see the heart sins beneath your behavioral sins, the idola-trous lies that drive you to do what you do. Remember, before you violate commandments 4–10, you violate commandments 1–3 by forsaking God for something else. When you see this, you begin to see how spiritually blind you have been. There is no more excuse making or blame-shifting; instead there is honest self-examination. You start to be self-critical with-out getting defensive or depressed.[12]

With that revelation of the sin beneath my sin, I fared much better in additional challenging conversations with my wife. Continually repenting of the deeper issue makes a huge difference in helping me avoid my typical passive-aggressive responses when I don't get my way.

Before you rule out anger as a sin issue in your life, make certain you have some idea of its many faces. It can take forms that deceive you. Its costs, as Robert Jones cautions, are high:

> Anger, in both its revealed and concealed forms, damages relationships. It severs marriages and alienates families. It keeps us from reconciling relationships and pursuing peace. Sinful anger excuses our planks and highlights others' specks (Matt. 7:3–5).[13]

6. Confess It

Once I yanked the plank out of my own eye, I had to ask my wife's forgiveness. Gratefully, I received it from her for the umpteenth time. When the Lord convicts us of a sin like anger, it's important that we own it. We must make amends with those we have offended. Don't leave things in the dark. Issues brought into the light lose their power over us (1 John 1:5–10). Keeping them in the dark by failing to confess and repent to others allows them to maintain their control over us.

I entered a Doctor of Ministry program back in the '90s. Our local seminary offered a class on church planting. It was just what I needed to get ready for starting a new church in Central Florida. No other core seminar in that curriculum proved more valuable to me. But the why behind that statement still surprises me to this day. A full one-half of the curriculum focused on the personal life of the church planter. I remember reading the class syllabus in advance and thinking, *Sounds like a waste of time to me. I want practical training in church planting*. Wrong! Dr. Jack Miller surgically sliced and diced my heart into a thousand pieces as he zeroed in on the character of the church planter. He pleaded with us about the priority of personal holiness. He exhorted us to deal decisively with sins in our lives like—you guessed it—anger. I remember weeping that day in class as the Holy Spirit nailed me about one relationship in particular. I knew I needed to address that person fast—before that Sunday, when we would end up worshiping the Lord together. Why? Let's get back to Jesus's teaching in Matthew 5 for more of his counsel on the matter.

Pursue Relational Reconciliation

Please be careful. Don't move through the text too quickly. Take another look at that first little word in Matthew 5:23, "So." It's another one of those cause-and-effect words in the Bible. Here's what you must do if unjustifiable anger poses such an enormous, even eternal, threat to your soul and the welfare of others: you must be a "do your best" peacemaker! Jesus gives two illustrations to press home the same idea. The best antidote to sins of anger is to commit to doing just the opposite—radical, immediate, determined, intentional, and vigorous peacemaking that reconciles relationships whenever and wherever possible. The examples involve two spheres of life—spiritual and civil—the church and the courthouse.

At the Altar in the Church

Jesus paints the first picture in a house of worship. "If you are offering your gift at the altar [historically, the Temple where the Jews came to offer sacrifices for their sins and to worship Yahweh would have housed the altar] and there remember that your brother has something against you, leave your gift there before the altar and go. First be reconciled to your brother, and then come and offer your gift" (vv. 23–24). This is stunning! Do you see what Jesus prescribes here? The need to do all necessary peacemaking with someone with whom your relationship has deteriorated trumps even your priority of corporate worship. First Samuel 15:22 reminds us: "to obey is better than sacrifice." It's hypocrisy to do otherwise. This is why many churches like ours "fence the table" with this warning. We are unfit for communion, or any other means of grace for that matter, if we are ducking our peacemaking responsibilities. "If possible, so far as it depends on you, live peaceably with all" (Rom. 12:18). Leslie Flynn offers helpful clarification:

> Jesus is not urging a habitual introspection at our worship services, nor is he suggesting that we postpone reconciliation till our regular Communion services. The point is that if we have delayed making peace, we would do well to postpone even the most solemn worship to go on a peace mission. Apparently worship will not be wholehearted if we are at odds with a brother. To reconcile is better than sacrifice, is Jesus's paraphrase of the Old Testament admonition to obey.[14]

On the Way to the Courts

Jesus draws his second illustration from the world, and the court system in particular. Here we are to imagine ourselves in a dispute of some kind with an adversary that has landed us on our way to see the judge. Jesus instructs with some very similar peacemaker counsel in Matthew 5:25: "Come to terms quickly with your accuser while you are going with him to court." Make every eager effort to settle the case. Even if it costs you! Charles Spurgeon advised, "A lean settlement is better than a fat lawsuit."[15]

Regardless of the scene, church or court, the message remains the same: the best antidote to anger gone viral is a sense of peacemaking urgency. Do everything you can possibly do, as quickly as you possibly can do it, in order to repair the breach in a relationship gone bad.

And if we don't, the consequences can be extraordinary. In the rest of this text, Jesus holds out the sobering prospect of a judgment in court, imprisonment, and fine-paying to the very last cent. Not a very pleasant picture. Ken Sande, in his book *The Peacemaker*, expands on this:

> Unresolved conflict can lead to many types of "prisons" and can exact penalties we never anticipate. In addition to robbing you of time, property, or money, prolonged conflict can damage your relationships and destroy your reputation. It can also imprison you in a dungeon of self-pity, resentment, or bitterness. . . . Ongoing hostility can destroy you from the inside and alienate you from God.[16]

Take Jesus's word for it. End up in his prison and you will never cease paying to the very last penny.

I can't stress enough the importance of this "come to terms quickly" peacemaking principle for excellence in safeguarding unity in our churches. If you want to stay ahead of anger and its destructive consequences in your church, you have to act fast in pursuing reconciliation. I learned the value of this in one of my early pastoral assignments. Not far from our church was a flagship megachurch in our affiliation pastored by one of the best-known Christian radio preachers of the day. Believe me, you would recognize the name if I told you. To my surprise, he graciously accepted an invitation to lunch one day. I opted to take a seminary intern with me for our mutual benefit. We enjoyed a thoroughly profitable time with the man.

Little did I know that I offended my board chairman in the process. Turns out he felt I should have invited him, not our seminary student, to share in that unique luncheon opportunity. And he may have been right! I made so many mistakes as a rookie pastor. It's a wonder I survived to tell this story. I don't know. He never granted me an opportunity to discuss it with him. He left the church over it. No manner of pleading by me or any of the other elders to get him to come to the table and work things out proved successful along the way. The end result left a good bit of wreckage in the church. We may well have avoided it if we both could have practiced a "first things first, be reconciled" peacemaking ethic with one another.

So, how do we respond to this teaching such that we can say we receive the broader implications of the sixth commandment? One, if you haven't done so, come to terms quickly with God—today, even (2 Cor. 7:1). He is the adversary with whom you and I must be most concerned. Repent of your sins, including anger, and believe in Jesus for your salvation.

Two, if the charge sticks, admit you're a rageaholic and declare war on your anger. Memorize and meditate upon Bible texts dealing with anger and its effects (see above). Get competent biblical counsel. Read up on the issue. Enlist the help of a friend. Attend an appropriate support group. Repent, believe the gospel, and obey. This is serious business we're talking about. Robert Jones is right: "People who cover over their anger must unlearn their avoidance style of managing conflict and develop new skills in Christlike reconciliation. . . . Peacemaking requires courageous expenditures of effort that exceed the natural comfort zone of concealers."[17]

Three, ask God for help with your anger. The Bible prescribes prayer for dealing with our anger. The apostle Paul made this connection in the pastoral epistles: "I desire then that in every place the men should pray, lifting holy hands without anger or quarreling" (1 Tim. 2:8). It's awfully tough to pray when you're jacked up with rage over someone or something they said or did. Martin Luther, the magisterial Reformer, offered a specific way to pray about anger in light of the sixth commandment. It involves both confession and petition.

> I confess and lament . . . that we do not acknowledge and will not learn such a commandment. . . . Instead, we despise it as though it does not

apply to us, or as though we have nothing to do with it. We . . . do not give it a second thought that when we despise our neighbor, we are acting contrary to this commandment. . . . We even murder him in our hearts. . . . We are like ferocious beasts walking all over one another, pushing, scratching, tearing, biting, and devouring one another, and we do not fear God's earnest command, etc.

I pray that our dear Father would instruct us to recognize His holy commandment and help us to hold to it and live accordingly. I pray that He would guard us all from the murderer, who is the master of all murder and harm, and give His rich grace, so that we will all be kind, gentle, and generous toward one another, heartily forgiving one another and bearing one another's mistakes and failings in a Christian and brotherly fashion. This is how we are to live together in genuine peace and unity, as this commandment teaches and demands of us.[18]

Four, pastors—douse outbursts of anger that may flare up in meetings. Exemplify the Holy Spirit's control (Gal. 5:19–24) yourselves when discussing difficult subjects. Call out in love and gentleness other brothers and sisters when things get overheated. We don't tolerate hotheads on our board. Elders are to be "self-controlled" (1 Tim. 3:2). Encourage all the robust debate you can to get to a wise decision on a matter, but never allow quarrelsome types in your midst (v. 3). When we have congregational meetings throughout the year, we often include what we call an "Ask Anything" time on the agenda. We invite our folks to bring up any subject they like about life at OGC. This is another way we strive to promote unity as a body, but it is risky business. People can get emotional about any number of issues related to their church. So I try to remind them to check unrighteous anger at the door, handle righteous indignation with care, and safeguard the unity of the church by how they raise questions about the ministry.

Five, everyone—fight anger with proactive peacemaking. Whatever anyone else might choose to do in this regard, determine that you will not ignore, procrastinate, or otherwise do an end-run on a relational conflict wherever it crops up. Keep short accounts. Refuse to allow offenses to accumulate over time. I see this problem occasionally in exit interviews with individuals who get frustrated with the church. When someone presents a backlog of multiple issues that have piled up for years, it normally proves impossible to overcome the negative cumulative effect. Folks inevitably move on. Please, please, take the initiative at the first sign of an offense that cannot be overlooked. Don't delay. Work for compromise along the way. Propose a settlement. Take a loss. Paul says in 1 Corinthians 6:7, "Why not rather suffer wrong?" particularly when it comes to taking a fellow Christian to court. We now turn in the next chapter to more on that particular obstacle to preserving peace in our churches.

6

Litigating

Staying in the Church—the Where of Settling Disputes

What causes quarrels and what causes fights among you? Is it not this, that your passions are at war within you? You desire and do not have, so you murder. You covet and cannot obtain, so you fight and quarrel. You do not have, because you do not ask. You ask and do not receive, because you ask wrongly, to spend it on your passions.

James 4:1–3

We are too ready to seek vindication or vengeance through adversary proceedings rather than peace through mediation. . . . Good Christians, just as they should be slow to anger, should be slow to sue.

Supreme Court Justice Antonin Scalia[1]

Concerning this second pitfall to preserving a church's peace, Pastor Ray Stedman shares a story from a time in his ministry:

The Apostle Paul is dealing with the problem of lawsuits among brethren in this passage from First Corinthians 6. Just last week, I picked up a current issue of a Christian magazine and read a report concerning two Christian organizations that are both involved in smuggling Bibles behind the Iron Curtain. They are now suing each other before the courts in libel actions for damages. As I read the article I could not help but wonder if they had spent any time reading the Bibles they smuggle, because here in this passage Paul very clearly says that kind of thing among believers is very definitely wrong.[2]

Indeed he does. Not just wrong, but, if I read Paul's tone correctly, ridiculously, scandalously, shamefully wrong—nothing short of "a disgraceful spectacle."[3] Check it out:

When one of you has a grievance against another, does he dare go to law before the unrighteous instead of the saints? Or do you not know that the saints will judge the world? And if the world is to be judged by you, are you incompetent to try trivial cases? Do you not know that we are to judge angels? How much more, then, matters pertaining to this life! So if you have such cases, why do you lay them before those who have no standing in the church? I say this to your shame. Can it be that there is no one among you wise enough to settle a dispute between the brothers, but brother goes to law against brother, and that before unbelievers? To have lawsuits at all with one another is already a defeat for you. Why not rather suffer wrong? Why not rather be defrauded? But you yourselves wrong and defraud—even your own brothers! (1 Cor. 6:1–8)

How much do you suppose the good folks at Corinth squirmed in their seats when this letter was read in church the day it arrived and they heard, "I say this to your shame" (v. 5)? In using a term like "shame," Paul invoked a sensitive motivation in confronting this particular symptom of the church's worldliness (3:3). Marion Soards notes, "Honor and shame were two of the most powerful cultural currents in antiquity."[4] They needed a good apostolic spanking and got it—for more than one reason too.

Let's just say that the Corinthians scored more of an F-minus than an A-plus on their preserving-peace report card. Unfortunately, they excelled at rivalries and divisions as a church, not unity and oneness. Paul confronted that issue early on in the letter, pleading, "I appeal to you, brothers, by the name of our Lord Jesus Christ, that all of you agree, and that there be no divisions among you, but that you be united in the same mind and the same judgment" (1 Cor. 1:10). Please note, however, Paul's affirmation of the Corinthians that preceded his confrontation of their sin:

> I give thanks to my God always for you because of the grace of God that was given you in Christ Jesus, that in every way you were enriched in him in all speech and all knowledge—even as the testimony about Christ was confirmed among you—so that you are not lacking in any gift, as you wait for the revealing of our Lord Jesus Christ, who will sustain you to the end, guiltless in the day of our Lord Jesus Christ. God is faithful, by whom you were called into the fellowship of his Son, Jesus Christ our Lord. (vv. 4–9)

No matter how much churches struggle with conflict that disrupts unity, leaders must always thank God for his grace in saving the members and consistently point them to the faithful God they love and serve. He and he alone can help us overcome the blind spots that foster disunity and division in our ranks.

A particularly challenging list of divisive matters at Corinth came in the form of believers hauling their fellow brothers and sisters in Christ before the secular courts to settle their disputes. These conflicts likely involved civil concerns—economic, property, fraud, and so forth—as opposed to criminal offenses.[5] That Paul forbids believers to rely on the civil magistrate in some respect is patently clear in this passage. But he does not mean to rule out that recourse for believers entirely. Paul himself appealed to Caesar (Acts 25:11). He wrote to another church regarding the state as ordained by God to bear the sword in punishing evil (Rom. 13:1–7). Civil governments do have realms of jurisdiction under which believers and unbelievers alike fall and to which we all must submit. For an excellent discussion of a more detailed analysis of these particulars, see Ken Sande's appendix in *The Peacemaker* entitled, "When Is It Right to Go to Court?"[6]

In the Greek culture that squeezed the church at Corinth into its worldly mold, everyone engaged in lawsuits so regularly that the habit was *one of their chief entertainments.*[7] If you think our world practices litigation to an extreme, take a look at the first-century legal madness that went on in the Greek world. Athenian law courts illustrate the major part of life litigation played among its citizens:

> If there was a dispute in Athens, the first attempt to settle it was by private arbitrator. In that event one arbitrator was chosen by each party, and a

third was chosen by agreement between both parties to be an impartial judge. If that failed to settle the matter, there was a court known as The Forty. The Forty referred the matter to a public arbitrator and the public arbitrator consisted of all Athenian citizens in their sixtieth year; and any man chosen as an arbitrator had to act whether he liked it or not under penalty of disenfranchisement. If the matter was not settled, it had to be referred to a jury court which consisted of two hundred and one citizens for cases involving less than about £50 and four hundred and one for cases involving more than that figure. There were indeed cases where juries could be as large as anything from one thousand to six thousand citizens.[8]

In stark contrast to the cultural norm, the Jews despised and forbade such tactics. Charles Hodge cites the rabbinic standard: "It is a statute which binds all Israelites, that if one Israelite has a cause against another, it must not be prosecuted before the Gentiles."[9] If you had a dispute with a fellow child of Abraham, you settled it before the rabbis in the synagogue and only in the synagogue. Christianity, as a movement, followed suit and churches adopted the same ethic. No wonder Paul sounds completely flabbergasted and dismayed at the prospect of the Corinthians aping the world in dragging one another off to court. And here he determines to put a stop to it—correcting yet another item in a seemingly unending list of peacemaking problems plaguing the Corinthian church.

Here's the main thing I believe the apostle argues with the strongest of words in this text: believers eager to preserve unity must reject, whenever possible, the scandalous folly of resolving their disputes before secular courts of law. Notice even the word choice in verse 1 that leads me to label the issue scandalous: "When one of you has a grievance against another [he assumes this will happen, as does Jesus in Luke 17:1–4], does he *dare* go to law before the unrighteous instead of the saints?" (1 Cor. 6:1, emphasis added). This really troubled the apostle. Alfred Poirier goes so far as to cast Paul's emotional state as one of outrage:

> Paul's anger rises to a fever pitch in verses 9–10 when he issues a strong warning against adulterers, homosexuals, idolaters, thieves, the greedy, slanderers, and swindlers as those who will not inherit God's kingdom. Surely Paul is associating the actions of the Corinthians who drag their

brothers and sisters into court with this list of those who live in deliberate and overt rebellion against God.[10]

Paul employs a favorite form of address to drive home his points. He poses a series of rapid-fire, rhetorical, sometimes biting, ironical, and even sarcastic questions designed to shame them out of the scandalous practice of suing one another (see v. 5). Along the way he cites three givens they should know that make such a practice ludicrously beyond belief for people serious about following King Jesus and protecting the peace and purity of their church.

Given #1: The Special Destiny of Judging for Believers

Paul opens his explanation for his dismay over their litigation-happy behavior by arguing theologically about the future.

> Or do you not know that the saints will judge the world? And if the world is to be judged by you, are you incompetent to try trivial cases? Do you not know that we are to judge angels? How much more, then, matters pertaining to this life! (vv. 2–3)

The first reason why believers should stay out of law courts as a rule just about takes your breath away. He says so much and yet with so little detail. More, Paul, please! Can't you elaborate here? For some reason he did not care to go any further than to say that, at the judgment and in the new creation, Jesus will in some way and to some degree delegate the responsibility of judging to saints—to those made righteous by Jesus's saving work on the cross. And if that is the case—that we will participate, either in simply observing (though I think he probably means more here) or by actually dispensing judgment, affairs in both the visible cosmos and the invisible realm of angels—how much more should we take responsibility to judge the affairs of this mundane, worldly, temporal life? His logic moves from the greater to the lesser to make his point. Ben Witherington summarizes:

> The Corinthians' problems arose not just from bad ethics or bad social value but from bad theology, which affected all worldly affairs and

matters including sexual and legal matters. They had an inadequate if not non-existent future eschatology, or at least future eschatology was not shaping their values and decision making. . . . If they are going to go on and judge the world, then surely they can handle an ordinary mundane matter now on their own.[11]

Daniel 7:21–22 speaks to this promise of our future involvement in judging:

> As I looked, this horn made war with the saints and prevailed over them, until the Ancient of Days came, and judgment was given for the saints of the Most High, and the time came when the saints possessed the kingdom.

Jesus promised the disciples in Luke 22:28–30 something similar:

> You are those who have stayed with me in my trials, and I assign to you, as my Father assigned to me, a kingdom, that you may eat and drink at my table in my kingdom and sit on thrones judging the twelve tribes of Israel.

Revelation 20:4 adds:

> Then I saw thrones, and seated on them were those to whom the authority to judge was committed. Also I saw the souls of those who had been beheaded for the testimony of Jesus and for the word of God, and those who had not worshiped the beast or its image and had not received its mark on their foreheads or their hands. They came to life and reigned with Christ for a thousand years.

Again, we are given precious little to go on in the way of detail for understanding just what this will entail, but the point still stands. We will judge in the next life; how can we eschew judging in this life? Theologian N. T. Wright argues, "People who believe that Jesus is already Lord and that he will appear again as judge of the world are called and equipped (to put it mildly) to think and act quite differently in the world from those who don't."[12] This holds true for judging disputes as much as any other aspect of our Christian lives—or at least it should.

Given #2: The Serious Disconnect with Adjudicating by Unbelievers

Paul then hammers the Corinthians with another question: "So if you have such cases, why do you lay them before those who have no standing in the church?" (1 Cor. 6:4). He gives a second reason why it makes no sense for believers to resort to the courts to resolve disputes. To do so is to lay the matter before those he termed "the unrighteous" back in verse 1. Many scholars think Paul's use of this term "unrighteous" voiced his concern over the prevailing corruption in the court system of the day. Preben Vang notes, "The courts of the local magistrates were downright rigged against the poor and the weak."[13] Chances of getting a just settlement, especially for the disenfranchised, made this controversy all the more troublesome within the fellowship.

The apostle may well have meant to include that in this indictment. It is difficult to say for sure. But at the very least he meant to communicate something like this: we are saints, the righteous, the justified. Why in the world would we want to hang out our dirty laundry before the pagan, the unrighteous, the unjustified? They have no standing in the church of the living God.[14] Bruce Winter clarifies:

> The reference to those of no account in the Christian "meeting" was to the outsider, i.e., the judge and the jury who presided over civil actions. They had no "status" in the Christian family, even though there were Christians who were all too conscious of the importance and the deference that should be given to their civic status as annually elected magistrates and jurors.[15]

Nonbelievers function on an entirely different basis, with a wholly different grid. This is utterly shameful (v. 5)! We're talking serious disconnect here, to say the least.

In the rest of verses 5 and 6, Paul hints at a largely ignored alternative to civil courts for believers needing to settle disputes, and he does so with yet another question. "Can it be that there is no one among you wise enough to settle a dispute between the brothers, but brother goes to law against brother, and that before unbelievers?" (Note the sanctified sarcasm as the Corinthians, like most Greeks, tended to boast of their wisdom [see 1 Cor. 3:18–20].) Inconceivable! Unimaginable! Preposterous!

Paige Patterson indicts the Corinthians for another damaging aspect of taking fights outside of the church for unbelievers to judge. "Such behavior placed the entire church under a cloud before the very people who were supposed to be the objects of its evangelistic and missionary endeavor."[16] The mission of the church to unreached people takes a hit when we do such a thing.

One of our elders, Chuck, once shared a story with me about how this principle influenced him to resist taking a fellow believer to court over a dispute. Chuck runs a commercial real estate business. In seeking a tenant for a long-time owner with which he enjoyed a good relationship, he had things get dicey over leasing a property of some significance. His commission would have been substantial. Finding a suitable renter proved problematic. At one point the client joined the process, an initiative not unwelcomed by Chuck. When they finally signed the lease with the new tenant, the owner pressed Chuck for a portion of his commission.

Though the contract clearly stated the entire 6 percent was to be paid to the company, Chuck acknowledged the owner's help and offered him two points. His outfit would settle for 4 percent. "Not good enough," said the owner. "I'll give you two and take four." Chuck knew he needed to dig deeper into a solution, so he called the man. The deal actually stood to profit a junior agent working for Chuck's company. He happened not to be a believer. The property owner openly professed Christ. When Chuck attempted to reason with the man about the fairness of their agreement, he argued that it would not be a good witness to his non-Christian employee to get so little in return for his efforts while working for a Christian property manager and his Christian client.

The owner was furious. "This has nothing to do with Christianity!" he protested. Chuck pushed back, "It has everything to do with our faith." But the man refused to budge. By rights, contractually, Chuck could have opted to take the owner to court for a settlement but he chose not to. He did not want that witness to affect his employee. Nor did he want to violate 1 Corinthians 6.

Did you see the hinted alternative in this section of the text? Someone "wise enough to settle a dispute between the brothers" (v. 5)? If you don't pursue resolving a squabble with a fellow believer outside the church in the courts, where do you do it? You do it inside the church, before wise and authoritative spiritual judges—before mediators, arbitrators, elders, or otherwise properly trained conciliators.

Jesus himself prescribed the procedure for doing this very thing within the church:

> If your brother sins against you, go and tell him his fault, between you and him alone. If he listens to you, you have gained your brother. But if he does not listen, take one or two others along with you, that every charge may be established by the evidence of two or three witnesses. *If he refuses to listen to them, tell it to the church*. And if he refuses to listen even to the church, let him be to you as a Gentile and a tax collector. Truly, I say to you, whatever you bind on earth shall be bound in heaven, and whatever you loose on earth shall be loosed in heaven. Again I say to you, if two of you agree on earth about anything they ask, it will be done for them by my Father in heaven. For where two or three are gathered in my name, there am I among them. (Matt. 18:15–20, emphasis added)

Now, of course, this presumes a church's leadership and people understand this. All must willingly embrace the responsibility. And it requires that one's "opponent," if he belongs to another church, will do the same. Nonetheless, the church should serve as the starting place for resolving disputes. Ken Sande explains why the church makes a superior venue to this end:

> Civil courts can make rulings on legal and property issues, but they have no jurisdiction or ability to address sin or other matters of the heart described. . . . Therefore, civil courts are completely powerless to resolve the root causes of a lawsuit or to help people break free from the sin that is fueling their dispute. . . . If the dispute involves matters of the heart, as almost all lawsuits do, God wants it resolved through the one institution he established to minister to the heart, which is the local church.[17]

Two additional factors must be noted about the courts as an inferior option:

> Two important elements would be missing. . . . The absence of the Spirit of God in the life of the arbiter [except in the case of a believer] would make it impossible for him to have the benefit of God's judgment; and . . . his consideration would extend no further than Roman law, thus failing to consider the law of God at many vital points.[18]

91

Given #3: The Shameful Defeat of Litigating against Family

Paul's campaign for change among the Corinthians in this area of shameful litigating peaks with its ramifications for them as family. You can't miss the emphasis on Christian brotherhood in this text, especially in the hard-hitting paragraph close: "But you yourselves [the Greek is emphatic] wrong and defraud—*even your own brothers*" (1 Cor. 6:8, emphasis added). To have a lawsuit before the court, let alone get a judgment, Paul calls "a defeat" (v. 7). It's a lose/lose proposition to haul a family member of the body of Christ into a court of law. Alan Johnson summarized Paul's judgment this way: "You have lost the case morally and spiritually before even going before a judge."[19]

In fact, it's so shameful a thing that Paul asks, "Why not rather suffer wrong? Why not rather be defrauded?" (v. 7). He gets in their face with a basic principle of Christian discipleship having to do with personal rights and the interests of others (Phil. 2:1–11). Craig Blomberg says it well:

> Whether inside or outside the church, the attitude of demanding one's rights remains diametrically opposed to Christ's teaching (Matt. 5:39–42) and example (1 Pet. 2:23). If two Christians cannot resolve their disagreements short of both secular litigation and Christian arbitration, something is fundamentally amiss. Better to suffer wrong—God will one day vindicate all injustices—than to alienate a fellow believer by requiring redress.[20]

Something *was* fundamentally amiss in Corinth. Paul minces no words: "You yourselves wrong and defraud" (1 Cor. 6:8)! The poor man is nearly beside himself with distress over this nonsense. It gets even scarier when he goes on to suggest that such behavior might class them among "the unrighteous"—not people who have been washed, sanctified, and justified in the name of the Lord Jesus Christ by the Spirit of God as they claimed to be (vv. 9–11). Please get this! There is a great deal at stake in the way we go about dealing with conflict. It says everything about our hearts and the lusts that control them. Often it reveals just how little the Spirit of Jesus and the gospel has control of them. Behave this way and we might as well cut a verse like this one out of our Bibles: "Do not repay evil for evil or reviling for reviling, but on the contrary, bless, for to this you were called, that you may obtain a blessing" (1 Pet. 3:9).

Dr. Harry A. Ironside used to tell this story from his past:

> Many years ago as a little fellow I attended a meeting in Toronto where some difficulty had come up between brethren and they did as the apostle suggests. My dear mother took me along. "Little pitchers have big ears," and I well remember how horrified I was to see men I esteemed and had been taught to respect apparently so indignant with each other. I can remember one man springing to his feet and with clenched fists saying, "I will put up with a good deal, but one thing I will not put up with, I will not allow you to put anything over on me; I will have my rights!" An old Scotch brother who was rather hard of hearing leaned forward holding his ear and said, "What was that, brother? I did not get that!" "I say, I will have my rights," said the man. "But you did not mean that, did you? Your rights? If ye had your rights, you would be in hell, wouldn't you? And you are forgetting—aren't you?—that Jesus did not come to get His rights, He came to get His wrongs, and He got them." I can still see that man standing there for a moment like one transfixed, and then the tears broke from his eyes and he said, "Brethren, I have been all wrong. Handle the case as you think best," and he sat down and put his face in his hands and sobbed before the Lord, and everything was settled in three minutes. When in this spirit it is so easy to clear things up; when we bow before the Lord, He straightens them out.[21]

"When in this spirit it is so easy to clear things up; when we bow before the Lord, He straightens them out." Yes, indeed. Believers eager to preserve the unity of the Spirit in the bond of peace must reject the ridiculous and audacious folly of resolving their disputes in secular courts of law. The special destiny of judging in the age to come commends it. The serious disconnect with adjudicating by unbelievers necessitates it. And the shameful defeat of litigating against family demands it.

Consider these practical takeaways from the principles in this passage of Scripture.

One, become a church member if you have not done so already. Conflict resolution through godly mediation and arbitration and church discipline is one of the privileges and responsibilities that membership affords. Think about it. There is nothing for you or your opponent to be put out of, if necessary, if you aren't already among those who have voluntarily put yourselves into it. In these litigious days, a church needs members' informed consent to hold them accountable to legitimate ecclesiastical authority.[22] Intentional commitment to the servant authority of godly leaders also helps leaders know before God for whom they are and are not accountable as shepherds "keeping watch over [their] souls" (Heb. 13:17).

Two, humbly approach your church leadership about the prospect of including peacemaking training resources in the church library, its bookstore, and/or as part of its Christian education program. In addition to the session on peacemaking in our membership class, our church regularly offers a semester-long class utilizing the DVD series *Resolving Everyday Conflict*.[23] This strategy affords an opportunity to communicate a thorough and robust peacemaking ethic in the local church.

I remember the first time I ever taught that class as part of the comprehensive Christian education plan for our church. Over seventy people showed up that first Sunday! We are an average-size church of about two hundred. We rarely see participation like that during the 9:30 preservice hour. But it spoke to both the real and felt need people have for training like this. We offer this class at least every three years in the plan's scope and sequence—more often if deemed necessary. I encourage your church to do the same.

Three, in personal conflict, if you can't overlook an offense, determine to follow as best you can the pattern of steps prescribed by Jesus in Matthew 18. Maintain in your thinking a high view of Christ's church. Keep matters there rather than taking them outside. Heed Richard Pratt's warning: "Because the church is so important and valuable, appealing to public courts demonstrates a lack of respect for God's holy institution, the church."[24] Be willing for wise, objective, and godly people to speak into your life along the way when they see something potentially out of order. Trust God to work through his appointed authority in pronouncing judgment when necessary.

Four, pastors, elders, shepherds, officers of the church—we simply must pay the price in helping our people stay in the church to settle their disputes. We must lay down our lives in painstaking due diligence to hear out the unresolved disputes brought before us. Nothing requires greater sacrifice in that regard than adjudicating church discipline cases.

To do this well requires much prayer, careful listening to all parties involved, long meetings, thorough investigation, meticulous note taking, and vigorous discussion in order to arrive at a wise decision. Let Paul's givens in the text constrain you to make room in your pastoral care for this kind of ministry in your church.

Five, study up even more on the subject of Christian conciliation and get familiar with other ministries that specialize in the same. Craig Blomberg cites a helpful reference to that end in the application section of his treatment of 1 Corinthians.[25]

Six, trust God and the gospel of grace and forgiveness to rule your relationships within the body of Christ. Behavior that chooses to suffer wrong, defrauding as opposed to coercing rights, doesn't come naturally to the sinful flesh. That takes the Fruit of the Spirit controlling the heart through the power of the gospel. Meditate often on texts like Philippians 2:1–11. If you feel you have been wronged and justice evades you for now, resolve never to seek vengeance. Refuse to take matters into your own hands. Put your hope in God's promises to right every wrong (Rom. 12:19–21).

John Calvin counseled in his *Institutes of the Christian Religion*, "Every man's best adviser is charity. Everything in which we engage without charity, and all the disputes which carry us beyond it, are unquestionably unjust and impious."[26] How much better it is to put on love in dealing with major issues like the offenses under discussion here and also in lesser ones over which we can suffer the disruption of peace. Such matters of conscience and difference of opinion are the focus of our next chapter.

7

Judging

Staying off the Throne—the Why of Settling Disputes

Judge not, that you be not judged. For with the judgment you pronounce you will be judged, and with the measure you use it will be measured to you.

Matthew 7:1–2

It is all too easy to fight and divide over peripheral matters of lifestyle and traditional religious practices. It is disgraceful that some Christians cannot praise God with their fellow brothers and sisters in worship because of disagreements over such "disputed matters." We must remember that "the kingdom of God is not a matter of eating and drinking but of righteousness and peace and joy in the Holy Spirit. . . . So then let us pursue what makes for peace and for mutual upbuilding (Rom. 14:17–19).

Alexander Strauch[1]

I have always felt that this little ditty hits a bit too close to home for comfort:

To live above with the saints we love, oh, how that will be glory.
To live below with the saints we know, now that's a different story.[2]

Quote that to any follower of Jesus invested in his church, and you will likely get a smile, wince, or both from a history of painful experience. One of the more problematic aspects of living "below with the saints we know" is our propensity for judging one another. This constitutes yet another serious pitfall for anyone desiring to make high grades in preserving peace in the body of Christ. As with the previous two land mines we've considered—anger and litigating—the New Testament gives us all the help we need for charting a course away from judging and toward a path of loving shaped by the gospel. I call it the grace of welcoming.

Once again we turn to the apostle Paul for help. His epistle to the Romans prescribes just what to do. Though I choose to introduce this discussion with Romans 15:7, "Therefore welcome one another as Christ has welcomed you, for the glory of God," please understand that it marks the climax of a prolonged argument reaching all the way back to Romans 14:1–4:

> As for the one who is weak in faith, welcome him, but not to quarrel over opinions. One person believes he may eat anything, while the weak person eats only vegetables. Let not the one who eats despise the one who abstains, and let not the one who abstains pass judgment on the one who eats, for God has welcomed him. Who are you to pass judgment on the servant of another? It is before his own master that he stands or falls. And he will be upheld, for the Lord is able to make him stand.

Here we encounter the same key word, first as a command, "As for the one who is weak in faith, *welcome* him" (v. 1, emphasis added). Then it occurs in a statement of fact, "for God has *welcomed* him" (v. 3, emphasis added). Whatever Paul means by "welcome," it matters greatly simply by the weight of emphasis he gives it. But before we dive into the particulars of these passages, let's get our bearings in terms of the letter's big picture.

Paul wrote his epistle to the Romans to prepare the church in that city for his coming visit. It easily contains his most thoroughgoing treatment/explanation of the gospel, which spans chapters 1 to 11. Beginning in chapter 12, he transitions from the indicative—what God has done for us in Jesus Christ—to the imperative—how we should then live in light of the glorious gospel. He covers a wide variety of relationships and issues as to how the gospel informs our choices with each. Then he lands in this final section on a special problem area for believers—passing judgment on one another—a serious threat to the harmony of the body of Christ. He prescribes this antidote for such a poison to genuine community: "welcome one another."

Paul's main point is this: the gospel shapes community by constraining us to manifest the grace of welcoming one another. In the text there are three things about this grace we need to grasp: the gist of welcoming, the ground of welcoming, and the goal of welcoming. My hope is that we will take Paul's counsel to heart in order to avoid this pitfall to preserving unity in our churches.

The Gist of Welcoming—Embracing

The gist of welcoming is an ongoing determination to embrace others in spite of differences over morally neutral matters. This does not apply to nonnegotiable items like the core beliefs of the Christian faith or the moral requirements of God's law. The issues involved here are of a secondary nature. They are matters of personal conscience and individual conviction only. Christina Cleveland underscores the extent to which dividing over such things impacts our churches, particularly among women:

> Christians are so good at erecting divisions that we don't stop at the major ones (e.g., race/ethnicity, class and gender); we also create divisions *within* divisions. For example, while the body of Christ experiences significant intergender (man vs. woman) division, it is also plagued by *intra*gender (woman vs. woman and man vs. man) division. For example, Christian women contribute to divisions between egalitarians and complementarians, stay-at-home moms and working moms (the infamous "Mommy Wars"), feminists and traditionalists, married women who take their husband's last name and married women who don't, unmarried and married women, urban and suburban women, black and white women, mothers and nonmothers, and young and old women, to name just a few.[3]

What a challenging list! Can you add to it from personal experience? I suspect you can. I've got a crazy-maker of my own to share later in this chapter—a mostly positive example. But I must admit that we've suffered our share of hits over this threat to unity.

Recently we solicited constructive inputs from a wide variety of folks who have left our church in recent years. We wanted help with a frank assessment about weaknesses we might possibly improve upon in the future. Talk about painful reading. I considered including one or more of the examples in this manuscript. I just couldn't bring myself to do so. Several things struck me, however, as I read through the feedback. The perception of judgmental, critical spirits within the congregation showed up more than I care to admit. Some of the comments even warranted an apology from me on behalf of our congregation. The whole exercise got me in touch with just how huge a threat critical spirits pose to the unity of a church. Pastors, don't underestimate this reality in your church. Pray against it, preach about it, and patiently confront it as you care for the flock and labor for its shalom.

Now, let's get back to the text for help in dealing with this pitfall. Paul speaks here of two different categories of believers in Rome. In Romans 14:1 he refers to those "weak in faith." In Romans 15:1 he talks of "we who are strong." Notice he counts himself among the strong by using the first-person plural "we." What does he mean? He gets very concrete in the next verse of chapter 14: "One person believes he may eat anything [the strong], while the weak person eats only vegetables" (14:2). Over the issue of food, these believers divided, probably not from a nutritional perspective but from a religious one. The vegetarians likely worried that eating meat might make them guilty of idolatry, if that meat came from offerings to idols (see 1 Cor. 8 for similar concerns in that fellowship). Apparently, the meat eaters lost no sleep over that so-called problem at all.

In the next paragraph, Paul introduces another area of controversy troubling the church:

> One person esteems one day as better than another, while another esteems all days alike. Each one should be fully convinced in his own mind. The one who observes the day, observes it in honor of the Lord. The one who eats, eats in honor of the Lord, since he gives thanks to God, while the one who abstains, abstains in honor of the Lord and gives thanks to God. (vv. 5–6)

"One person esteems one day as better than another, while another esteems all days alike" (v. 5). In both matters of eating and day-keeping, both groups do as they do for the same motive. They desire to honor God (v. 6). Each cares supremely about pleasing God. This is all-important. One is not wrong and the other right. Nonetheless, Paul does distinguish between the contrasting convictions with the words "strong" and "weak." By "strong" he means the spiritually mature, fully able to enjoy their Christian liberty—completely emancipated from unchristian inhibitions and taboos. By "weak," he means the spiritually less mature. The believers in this camp are not yet fully liberated by the gospel and its call to freedom (see Gal. 5:13). Rather they are constrained in their consciences not to do certain things for fear of displeasing God. Jim Boice illustrated strong and weak with this example:

> Charles Spurgeon was the greatest preacher of his age, but he was frequently criticized for being funny. When one woman objected to the humor he inserted into his sermons Spurgeon told her, "Madam, you would think a great deal better of me if you knew the funny things I kept out."
>
> A young man asked what he should do about a box of cigars he had been given. Spurgeon solved his problem. "Give them to me," he said, "and I will smoke them to the glory of God."
>
> On another occasion Spurgeon was criticized for traveling to meetings in a first class railway carriage. His antagonist said, "Mr. Spurgeon, what are you doing up here? I am riding back there in the third class carriage taking care of the Lord's money." Spurgeon replied, "And I am up here in the first class carriage taking care of the Lord's servant."[4]

Guess which category Spurgeon allowed himself to enjoy?

Here's the problem. In Rome, both sides—strong and weak—took one another to task over their respective stances. "Let not the one who eats despise the one who abstains, and let not the one who abstains pass judgment on the one who eats" (Rom. 14:3). The Greek word for "despise" is a strong word. It means to consider as nothing, to treat with contempt. The strong who ate judged the weak who did not eat as legalists; the weak who abstained judged the strong who chowed down as libertines. That kind of critical judgment built walls between the two factions in the community and created chasms in their fellowship. And to that Paul strongly objected, giving this command: "welcome one another" (15:7).

The Greek word means literally "to take to oneself." It's the idea of "accept" or "receive." I like the word *embrace*. Perhaps one of the best concrete biblical examples we have of the spirit behind the word comes from Paul's shipwreck on Malta: "The native people showed us unusual kindness, for they kindled a fire and *welcomed* us all, because it had begun to rain and was cold" (Acts 28:2, emphasis added). To "welcome" is to draw someone into your fellowship and companionship, to treat them gently and kindly, irrespective of their views on morally neutral issues—and not, by the way, for the purpose of disputing about those things! Paul makes that patently clear right out of the chute: "Welcome him, but not to quarrel over opinions" (Rom. 14:1). Forget that and do this instead: "Each one should be fully convinced in his own mind" (v. 5).

If you want to do the best you can to preserve unity in your church, you have to learn to think this way: *Mine is not to change my brother's mind; mine is to embrace my brother.* We must do that whether he is strong or weak, eating or not, drinking or not, smoking or not, movie- and theater-going or not, and a host of other so-called gray areas, doubtful things, or principles of conscience the Scripture does not color in black-and-white. So the gist of welcoming as a gospel-shaped community is an ongoing determination to embrace others in spite of differences over morally neutral matters.

May I boast about my own church on this front for a bit? During the writing of this book, I lost my wife of nearly forty-two years to a battle with cancer. I loved Nancy. And the people of Orlando Grace Church treasured her as well. She and I enjoyed a terrific marriage. It was hard to watch her suffer. I am grateful to know, however, that she left me for a better Man! As I finished the bereavement leave graciously granted to me by the church, I returned to full-time ministry, by God's grace, with more gratitude than grief affecting my everyday experience. Now, brace yourself for the potential crazy-maker and largely positive example I hinted at earlier in this chapter: within ten months I remarried.

Yes, not a year passed before I wed my second wife. God had brought Jan, a very special, godly woman, into our church as a covenant member three years earlier. There is a lot to our love story in the way the Lord brought us together that I won't get into here. But, as you might imagine, the relative speed with which I moved toward her after losing my first wife raised some eyebrows. By and large our people embraced me and Jan. They refused to judge our hearts. They gave us the benefit of the doubt. Many even cheered us on. One brother even told me, "I prayed for this—I just didn't think it would happen so fast!"

Now, I won't kid you. Some of our folks did struggle with this—especially, and understandably so, a few of our women. With the Lord's help we turned the matter into another opportunity to flex our peacemaking muscles. One dear sister came to me admitting her difficulty with the whole idea. We talked it through. The next Sunday I shared from the pulpit how loved I felt by her approaching me. I invited anyone else with similar concerns to reach out to me. A few more conversations followed. They yielded similar peaceful results. But in the end I was so proud of our people for the grace of nonjudgment they demonstrated in our community. Other pastors should be so fortunate.

The Ground of Welcoming—the Gospel and Judgment of God

The apostle Paul anchors his argument for refusing critical judgment in two grand spiritual truths: the gospel of God who has welcomed us in Jesus Christ and the judgment of God before which every believer ultimately stands or falls. The first is so important that Paul says it twice. Each time he invokes a different member of the Trinity to support his case. Why should neither the strong nor weak despise or pass judgment on the other? Answer involving the Father: "for God has welcomed him" (Rom. 14:3). Answer involving the Son, the conclusion of the matter: "Therefore welcome one another as Christ has welcomed you, for the glory of God" (15:7).

The grace for preserving oneness in the church flows from the grace of God in the gospel and his great love for us. The ground for obedience does not differ at all from the ground for forgiveness: "Be kind to one another, tenderhearted, forgiving one another, as God in Christ forgave you" (Eph. 4:32).

Don't miss this. In one respect, Paul's way of reasoning is from the lesser to the greater. And here's why. Consider his thinking earlier in the letter:

> For while we were still *weak*, at the right time Christ died for the *ungodly*. For one will scarcely die for a righteous person—though perhaps

for a good person one would dare even to die—but God shows his love for us in that while we were still *sinners*, Christ died for us. Since, therefore, we have now been justified by his blood, much more shall we be saved by him from the wrath of God. For if while we were *enemies* we were reconciled to God by the death of his Son, much more, now that we are reconciled, shall we be saved by his life. (Rom. 5:6–10, emphasis added)

All Jesus asks of us in a gospel-shaped, peacemaking community is to welcome believers with differing opinions on the gray areas of the Christian life. That's the lesser. How tough can that be (here comes the greater) for we whom the Father and the Son welcomed, received, embraced, justified, adopted, and loved? We were not just weak but ungodly, sinners, and enemies! Matthew Henry said it so well:

> Can there be a more cogent argument? Has Christ been so kind to us, and shall we be so unkind to those that are his? Was he so forward to entertain us, and shall we be backward to entertain our brethren? Christ has received us into the nearest and dearest relations to himself: has received us into his fold, into his family, into the adoption of sons, into a covenant of friendship, yea, into a marriage-covenant with himself; he has received us (though we were strangers and enemies, and had played the prodigal) into fellowship and communion with himself.[5]

As if the good news of God in Jesus Christ was not enough to convict us about the virtue of welcoming others, Paul throws fuel on the fire with a second motivation—the judgment of God before which every believer ultimately stands or falls. Did you catch this? "Who are you to pass judgment on the servant of another? It is before his own master that he stands or falls" (14:4).

Paul likens the temptation to judge another believer about doubtful things to meddling in the household affairs between masters and servants. Servants in the first century lived in the homes of their masters as part of the family. They gave account to their own masters and to their own masters only. For anyone to presume to judge a brother or sister on a morally neutral matter would be like the master or slave of one household butting into the affairs of a master or slave of another. It's not our business. Then whose business is it? God's! Paul hammers the same thing again later in the chapter so we don't miss the point:

Why do you pass judgment on your brother? Or you, why do you despise your brother? For we will all stand before the judgment seat of God; for it is written,

"As I live, says the Lord, every knee shall bow to me,
    and every tongue shall confess to God."

So then each of us will give an account of himself to God. (vv. 10–12)

Does this point grip us? Exercise maximum care here. Judging another presumes to put ourselves in God's place. We do not want to go there, especially when we absorb how Paul concludes: "And he will be upheld, for the Lord is able to make him stand" (v. 4). You and I may be ready to pronounce someone's standing or falling before God because of our differing personal preference. But grapple with this before you bring down the hammer on your brother or sister: God will uphold him—make him stand before him and not fall—because the person acts in accord with his informed conscience on that matter as best as he understands. Never forget. God's power guards them (1 Pet. 1:5), and God is the one able to keep them from stumbling and make them stand (Jude 24). Beware of usurping the place of God in another believer's life.

John Piper stresses how much rides on taking care to calculate both grounds for embracing others with differing convictions:

When your life extends and channels the forgiving grace of God in Christ to others, it's plain that you are the recipient of the forgiving grace of Christ. . . . The merciful will receive mercy in the judgment, not because mercy earns mercy, but because treating others with the mercy of Christ shows you have received and trusted the mercy of Christ. Your name is in the book. But if you judge and judge and judge with no brotherly affection, or if you despise your fellow believer with no brotherly affection . . . then you should tremble and seek to confirm by faith in Christ that your name is written in the book of life.[6]

The Goal of Welcoming—the Glory of God

Paul pulls out all the stops in concluding his war on judging in the fellowship. He implies that nothing less than God's glory hangs in the balance with the harmony and unity of his church. Back to the climactic verse: "Therefore welcome one another as Christ has welcomed you." Why? "For the glory of God" (Rom. 15:7).

This connects in the immediate context to the benediction Paul inserts in verses 5–6:

> May the God of endurance and encouragement grant you to live in such harmony with one another, in accord with Christ Jesus, that together you may with one voice glorify the God and Father of our Lord Jesus Christ.

Did you see the "therefore" at the beginning of Romans 15:7? In light of Paul's prayer for them, *therefore* they should welcome one another. As Warren Wiersbe observed: "The neighbors were watching!"[7] A welcoming, receiving, embracing spirit toward those who differ with us on some of these thorny issues speaks volumes to the praise and glory of God before a watching world. Paul does not concern himself as much with who is right or wrong. That's not the point. It's how we treat one another. His preeminent concern is that we guard the peace, unity, and harmony of the community and thus safeguard the Lord's reputation before the eyes of an often skeptical and cynical world.

Let me ask you some candid questions as this chapter comes to a close. First, how welcoming a Christian are you? Be honest now, please. Think about your preferences of conscience—especially the ones about which you feel most strongly. Do they stand between you and anybody else in the body of Christ? Do you look askance at, keep your distance from, or otherwise shun someone for a contrary perspective? If so, I beg of you: give it up. Your judgment of the weak or strong hinders the peace of your congregation. Determine to distinguish accurately between primary and secondary issues in your fellowship. Ask forgiveness of anyone you have judged inappropriately in this regard.

Second, which category of Christian bests fits you when it comes to disputable matters, weak or strong? If the former more accurately describes your approach, see yourself for what the Bible calls you—weak! You've yet to grow into a measure of freedom granted everyone in the gospel. If the latter is the case with you, don't get cocky with your freedom. Don't flaunt it at the expense of the weaker members of the family. Be patient with them. Pray. Coach them in the gospel, as you have opportunity, that they might mature in navigating these issues like you have by God's grace.

Third, what might help you to appreciate more thoroughly the grace of the gospel and the weight of God's judgment for cultivating a more welcoming spirit with others? Consider reading through Romans and Galatians several times. Study with another friend or group some of the excellent resources about the gospel on the bookshelf these days.[8] Memorize and meditate upon some key passages of Scripture that emphasize future judgment.[9]

Fourth, have you made the connection between the unity within your church and the glory of God on display in the community around you? Francis Schaeffer called this the final apologetic in the church's defense of the faith before unbelievers. Based on John 17:21–23, where Jesus prayed for his followers, Schaeffer wrote:

> Now comes the sobering part. Jesus goes on in this 21st verse to say something that always causes me to cringe. If as Christians we do not cringe, it seems to me we are not very sensitive or very honest, because Jesus here gives us the final apologetic. What is the final apologetic? "*That they all may be one;* as thou, Father, art in me and I in thee, that they also may be one in us: *that the world may believe that thou hast sent me.*" This is the final apologetic. . . . We cannot expect the world to believe that the Father sent the Son, that Jesus's claims are true, and that Christianity is true, unless the world sees some reality of the oneness of true Christians. . . . Now that is frightening.[10]

It should be frightening and make us cringe. God's glory and the validity of the faith, humanly speaking, hang in the balance on how well we love one another and refrain from judging.

At the 1996 Promise Keepers Pastors' Conference in the Georgia Dome, I actually heard pastor and author Max Lucado present this masterful piece called "Life Aboard the Fellow-Ship."

> God has enlisted us in his navy and placed us on his ship. The boat has one purpose—to carry us safely to the other shore.
>
> This is no cruise ship; it's a battleship. We aren't called to a life of leisure; we are called to a life of service. Each of us has a different task. Some, concerned with those who are drowning, are snatching people

PART THREE

Mastering the Practices That Foster Unity in Jesus's Church

8

Intercepting Relational Disasters before They Ever Occur

Do nothing from selfish ambition or conceit, but in humility count others more significant than yourselves. Let each of you look not only to his own interests, but also to the interests of others.

Philippians 2:3–4

What makes saintliness in my view, as distinguished from ordinary goodness, is a certain quality of magnanimity and greatness of soul that brings life within the circle of the heroic.

Harriet Beecher Stowe[1]

I umpired Little League baseball for ten years. Both my sons played ball. I coached them their first year, and saw that way too many games suffered for lack of competent officials, so I decided I would take matters into my own hands. I changed roles from coach to umpire. I started calling balls and strikes, fair and foul, safe and out, the very next year. I loved it. I know, it sounds crazy. Who likes doing a volunteer job when half the crowd hates you for every close decision you make? Chalk it up to my control issues. In the immortal words of one-time National League umpire Auggie Moran, "They may be balls—they may be strikes. But until I call them—they ain't nothin'."[2]

Officiating the complex game of baseball well does not come easy. Every season I attended clinics around the state of Florida to hone the skills and master the mechanics. I worked my way up the ranks, eventually earning a spot in the rotation at the Southeast Regional tournament in St. Pete in 1997. In fact, if Florida hadn't been one of the finalists in the championship game, I would have worked the dish (home plate) on ESPN2. I sat in the stands with the rest of the fans (which was undoubtedly good for my humility). But the hard work paid off. I would like to think my commitment to excellence as a volunteer umpire made a difference in the joy of the kids playing ball on my watch.

Throughout our journey through *The Peacemaking Church*, I have sought to cast a vision for excellence in peacemaking that works hard to preserve the gift of church unity. So far we have looked at the priorities of such a peacemaker and the pitfalls to avoid along the way. Just as officiating any sport with excellence requires mastery of certain practices on the field, safeguarding unity requires mastery of certain practices in the church. Part 3 will now focus on two commitments do-your-best peacemakers must master in their congregations. The first involves the skill of heading off relational train wrecks before they ever occur.

I cannot verify the source of this account and cannot even be entirely certain it happened. But it well illustrates the main idea behind this chapter.

> One day a beggar by the roadside asked for alms from Alexander the Great as he passed by. The man was poor and wretched and had no claim upon the ruler, no right even to lift a solicitous hand. Yet the Emperor threw him several gold coins. A courtier was astonished at his generosity and commented, "Sir, copper coins would adequately meet a beggar's need. Why give him gold?" Alexander responded in royal fashion, "Copper coins would suit the beggar's need, but gold coins suit Alexander's giving."[3]

The Emperor insisted on a level of giving befitting his generous heart. The Old Testament contains a similar example of extravagant spirit in Genesis 13:1–13.

> So Abram went up from Egypt, he and his wife and all that he had, and Lot with him, into the Negeb.
> Now Abram was very rich in livestock, in silver, and in gold. And he journeyed on from the Negeb as far as Bethel to the place where his tent

had been at the beginning, between Bethel and Ai, to the place where he had made an altar at the first. And there Abram called upon the name of the LORD. And Lot, who went with Abram, also had flocks and herds and tents, so that the land could not support both of them dwelling together; for their possessions were so great that they could not dwell together, and there was strife between the herdsmen of Abram's livestock and the herdsmen of Lot's livestock. At that time the Canaanites and the Perizzites were dwelling in the land.

Then Abram said to Lot, "Let there be no strife between you and me, and between your herdsmen and my herdsmen, for we are kinsmen. Is not the whole land before you? Separate yourself from me. If you take the left hand, then I will go to the right, or if you take the right hand, then I will go to the left." And Lot lifted up his eyes and saw that the Jordan Valley was well watered everywhere like the garden of the LORD, like the land of Egypt, in the direction of Zoar. (This was before the LORD destroyed Sodom and Gomorrah.) So Lot chose for himself all the Jordan Valley, and Lot journeyed east. Thus they separated from each other. Abram settled in the land of Canaan, while Lot settled among the cities of the valley and moved his tent as far as Sodom. Now the men of Sodom were wicked, great sinners against the LORD.

The bulk of the chapter concerns a dispute between Abram's and Lot's herdsmen brewing in the south forty. It resulted in a negotiated agreement between the two heads of households. Abram demonstrates a remarkable example of spiritual largesse that can only be described as magnanimous. In so doing he intercepts a family conflict before it ever takes its toll on their relationship.

Magnanimity's Secret

Before examining that in detail, notice how the text begins and ends. Here is an insight, perhaps a secret, which explains why Abram could respond the way he did in this mess with his nephew. The first verse sets the stage: "So Abram went up from Egypt, he and his wife and all that he had, and Lot with him, into the Negeb" (13:1). In Genesis 12:10–20, Abram had barely escaped from disaster with Pharaoh down in Egypt. Overtaken by unbelief, he concocted a half-truth scheme about Sarai, his wife, being his sister. He feared for his own life as a stranger living in Egypt because of the severe famine in Canaan. The king took Sarai

115

to make her the next prize in his harem. That move resulted in God preserving his promised blessing through Abram (vv. 1–3) by bringing horrendous plagues upon Pharaoh and his entire household. When the king finally got the picture, he confronted Abram big-time. He literally threw Abram and Sarai out of Egypt.

So that explains the return to the Negeb at the outset of the chapter. It is no accident that these accounts come back-to-back. In chapter 12, blessing's bearer to the nations—as I like to call him—breaks down miserably with the Pharaoh debacle. In chapter 13 he gets back on track spiritually with his own extended household. To me the crucial difference between the two situations and their respective outcomes is revealed in verses 3–4.

> And he journeyed on from the Negeb as far as Bethel to the place where his tent had been at the beginning, between Bethel and Ai, to the place where he had made an altar at the first. And there Abram called upon the name of the LORD.

This is reminiscent of Abram's behavior back in Genesis 12:4–9, where he went about Canaan building altars for a strategic purpose. Did you see it at the end of verse 4? "Abraham called upon the name of the LORD." It appears Abram learned a lesson from his failures of Genesis 12:10–20. He sought God again. He returned to the business of altar building—calling upon God in prayer. It makes all the difference in the world. This is a huge turning point in how chapter 12 ends and how chapter 13 unfolds—the marked contrast vividly plain between things with Pharaoh and things with Lot. But there's more.

Notice the end of the chapter. It follows Lot and Abram's mutually agreed upon parting as a result of their negotiations. "So Abram moved his tent and came and settled by the oaks of Mamre, which are at Hebron, and there he built an altar to the LORD" (13:18). This chapter begins with altar building and it ends with altar building. It seems like we have two different characters here. We want to ask about the man in Genesis 13, "Who are you, and what have you done with the Abram of Genesis 12?" The contrast could hardly be more striking. A renewed God-centered orientation in chapter 13 enables Abram with great grace to head off a near relational train wreck with Lot.

We have to get this big idea. This is crucial for excellence in preserving unity in our churches. A God-centered lifestyle manifests itself in a genuinely magnanimous spirit in dealing with potential relational disasters. *Magnanimous* is defined this way: "generous or forgiving, especially towards a rival or less powerful person."[4] The secret for dispensing blessing as a magnanimous spirit, particularly when we are insulted or disrespected, lies in the supernatural resource of a God-centered, altar-building, "walk by faith, not by sight" (2 Cor. 5:7) lifestyle.

Let me state the obvious. Magnanimity is not a natural virtue. Our flesh wants nothing to do with characteristics like humility, meekness, forgiveness, or forbearance. Everything within us wars against such saintliness. It takes supernatural help to choose a different way—Abram's versus Lot's. The writer means for us to take serious note of the contrast. Only a Spirit-filled walk (Gal. 5:16–26) will enable us to manifest consistently that kind of spiritual magnanimity in dealing with conflict. This may be especially true about wealth. There just simply isn't enough room for everybody and his possessions in Genesis 13. And there is an underlying tension running throughout the account. What is to become of God's promise to Abram about this land over which its multiple inhabitants appear just about to implode? Abram heads disaster off at the pass by manifesting six different aspects of a magnanimous spirit.

Before examining these important qualities of magnanimity, let me ask you an all-important question: How goes your altar building these days? Would you say that, more than not, you are making God the center of your existence (Ps. 37:4) through a variety of means?[5] For example, are you consistently staying close to Jesus—abiding in the vine—through regular reading of God's Word and the practice of intercessory prayer (John 15:1–8)? Do you make a weekly priority of attendance at corporate worship to sit under the preaching of the gospel, feast at the communion table, and fellowship with God's people (Heb. 10:24–25)? Are you filled with the Spirit of God, walking in his power, as opposed to being controlled by your flesh (Gal. 5:16–26; Eph. 5:18–21)? Puritan commentator Matthew Henry spoke about the need for altar building on both special occasions and as a constant practice:

> Abram attended on God in his instituted ordinances. He built an altar unto the Lord who appeared to him, and called on the name of the Lord. Now consider this, (1.) As done upon a special occasion. When God appeared to him, then and there he built an altar, with an eye to the God who appeared to him. . . . Thus he acknowledged, with thankfulness,

God's kindness to him in making him that gracious visit and promise; and thus he testified his confidence in and dependence upon the word which God had spoken. . . . (2.) As his constant practice, whithersoever he removed. As soon as Abram had got to Canaan, though he was but a stranger and sojourner there, yet he set up, and kept up, the worship of God in his family; and wherever he had a tent God had an altar, and that an altar sanctified by prayer. . . . Note, those that would approve themselves the children of faithful Abram, and would inherit the blessing of Abram, must make conscience of keeping up the solemn worship of God, particularly in their families, according to the example of Abram. The way of family worship is a good old way, is no novel invention, but the ancient usage of all the saints. Abram was very rich and had a numerous family, was now unsettled and in the midst of enemies, and yet, wherever he pitched his tent, he built an altar. Wherever we go, let us not fail to take our religion along with us.[6]

Are you building an altar wherever you pitch your tent? Are you taking your religion with you wherever you go? Let me challenge you right here and now. If you can't honestly say yes to these questions—if you are doing more monument building to yourself versus altar building to God—put this book down and talk candidly with the Lord. Admit you've lost your way. Abram got off track. It happens to a lot, if not most, of us at one time or another. You're not the first. You won't be the last. Ask the Lord to help you climb back out of your personal Egypt. Plead with him to lead you up to your version of the Negeb to seek him again as the utmost priority of your life (Col. 3:1–4). Your hope and mine of demonstrating the six aspects of relational magnanimity depend upon a radical God-centered lifestyle locked in on him like a laser.

1. Taking Initiative to Defuse Tension

The conflict begins among the herdsmen. It does not start with Lot and Abram; it crops up among their servants. It concerned the tensions created by the amount of property managed by each man's workers. Additionally, verse 7 tells us about the presence of hostile Canaanites and Perizzites crowding the territory as well. Word about the dispute eventually got to the owners. Someone reported back to base concerning the escalating tensions in the field.

But verse 8 is clear: "Then Abram said to Lot." The uncle took the first step. So often conflict occurs because, in pride, fear, selfishness, or all of the above, no one will take the initiative. No one will start to move the logjam. Neither will humble himself, take the risk, and venture to communicate something like, "Hey, we have to deal with this." And yet this is precisely what the Scripture calls us to do in verses such as Romans 12:18: "If possible, *so far as it depends on you*, live peaceably with all" (emphasis added). How many relational disasters might be averted if someone could just say, "I'm going to be the one to take the first step to talk about the problem at hand." Initiative fosters magnanimity.

2. Making Effort to Avoid Arguments

Abram's words reveal his heart: "Then Abram said to Lot, 'Let there be no strife between you and me, and between your herdsmen and my herdsmen, for we are kinsmen'" (v. 8). Allow me to rephrase: "Lot, we're family. We're flesh and blood, son. You're my nephew; I'm your uncle. I don't want any strife between us." Do you see the value driving Abram in terms of his initiative? He will avoid a conflict—not at any cost—he learned that in Egypt. He was a "peacefaker" there. Here he is a true peacemaker. He will pay any reasonable cost—perhaps even an unreasonable one. But he will do so because he prizes the relationship above all else. He will avoid a breach if he can do anything at all to prevent it. He models ancient wisdom: "The beginning of strife is like letting out water, so quit before the quarrel breaks out" (Prov. 17:14). The word picture here reminds me of the vivid images of 2005 coming out of New Orleans with Hurricane Katrina, when the rising waters breached the levees in that city. Abandon the argument before the quarrel breaks out and potentially drowns the relationship.

King Solomon calls this proactive strategy a highly desirable virtue. "It is an honor for a man to keep aloof from strife, but every fool will be quarreling" (20:3). Bruce Waltke, in his commentary on Proverbs, comments: "The wise are more concerned to bring peace than to be right. But the fool cannot restrain himself and at the first opportunity explodes and shows his teeth."[7] I don't think Dr. Waltke means to imply that it would be right in the name of peacemaking to deny a black-and-white biblical principle. I think he's talking more about gray areas (see chapter 7) where one could conceivably yield and bend without sacrificing integrity. In those instances a fool's need to be right trumps wisdom's concern to keep peace in a relationship. The demeanor required for this kind of wisdom is magnanimous, not hotheaded.

When my wife Nancy passed away, many people paid tribute for the way she had made a difference in their lives. Most of them focused on her contribution to their physical health as a naturopathic practitioner. But Nancy did her share of marital counseling with me in the ministry as well. One woman went out of her way to share a word of exhortation from Nan that she never forgot: "You care more about being right than you do the oneness of your marriage." To this day the woman credits that single observation for turning things around in her troubled relationship with her husband. Since then, oneness has mattered more than winning arguments in that home.

3. Declining Rights to Press Advantages

Abram appealed to Lot as his kinsman (v. 8). Family values mattered greatly from his perspective. Would anyone have blamed him if he responded more like this: "I'm your uncle, you little ungrateful so-and-so. What do you think you're doing? You've got a lot of nerve, after all I have done for you." He was the clan leader. He was wealthier. Lot owed everything to him for bringing him up from Ur (see Gen. 11:31). Lot will owe him again in the daring rescue coming in Genesis 14. But that clearly isn't the card Abram played. He engaged him equal to equal. His brotherly affection spilled over onto Lot in spades.

The Scriptures appeal to us over and over again to treat one another with extravagant love precisely because Jesus has made us brothers and sisters:

Love one another with brotherly affection. (Rom. 12:10)

Now concerning brotherly love you have no need for anyone to write to you, for you yourselves have been taught by God to love one another. (1 Thess. 4:9)

Let brotherly love continue. (Heb. 13:1)

120

Honor everyone. Love the brotherhood. (1 Pet. 2:17)

For this very reason, make every effort to supplement your faith with virtue, and virtue with knowledge, and knowledge with self-control, and self-control with steadfastness, and steadfastness with godliness, and godliness with brotherly affection, and brotherly affection with love. (2 Pet. 1:5–7)

Clothe yourselves, all of you, with humility toward one another. (1 Pet. 5:5)

Abram wore his lowliness outfit on this occasion. He did not press his rights. He played no status card to leverage the advantage. He ferociously guarded peace, because the welfare of his household hung in the balance. Alfred Poirier presses the importance of this dynamic in our churches from a church leadership angle:

We as pastors and other church leaders are not to think of our people merely as members. . . . There is a direct correspondence between how we reduce them to mere people filling the pews and our lack of true table fellowship with them. . . . We can begin to seek genuine peace when we learn to regard our people as brothers and sisters in the Lord.[8]

4. Making Choices to Release Control

Abram's magnanimity and spiritual resolve shine brilliantly in the story. "Is not the whole land before you? Separate yourself from me. If you take the left hand, then I will go to the right, or if you take the right hand, I will go to the left" (v. 9). Our culture and time would probably pull Abram aside and question his sanity. We would advise him to think more than twice about such an offer. This is remarkable. "You choose, my boy. I'll take the leftovers." Is this not the spirit of our study two chapters ago? "To have lawsuits at all with one another is already a defeat for you. Why not rather suffer wrong? Why not rather be defrauded?" (1 Cor. 6:7). This has James 3:17–18 written all over it:

But the wisdom from above is first pure, then peaceable, gentle, open to reason, full of mercy and good fruits, impartial and sincere. And a harvest of righteousness is sown in peace by those who make peace.

121

Here's how you measure your wisdom quotient. Apply the kind of checklist commended here:

> Finally, all of you, have unity of mind, sympathy, brotherly love, a tender heart, and a humble mind. Do not repay evil for evil or reviling for reviling, but on the contrary, bless, for to this you were called, that you may obtain a blessing. (1 Pet. 3:8–9)

The biggest challenge I encounter in conflict coaching and mediation is convincing people to choose blessing instead of reviling. Tim Lane and Paul Tripp probe the reason behind this dynamic:

> Why do we struggle to rejoice at another's blessing? . . . *We want our own way, in the way we have chosen, and at the time we have deemed best.* We love us and have a wonderful plan for our lives! We have a dream. The problem is that it is not the Lord's.[9]

Abram chose a different way. He sought Lot's interests over his own (Phil. 2:3–4). And he did so for good reason.

5. Having Courage to Accept Outcomes

For Abram to offer first choice to his nephew took guts. And there is no hint of Lot countering with a similar spirit of deferment. At this point there is something terribly important to observe in the text. In response to Abram's magnanimous offer, the Bible tells us this: "Lot lifted up his eyes" (Gen. 13:10). He gazed upon well-watered Jordan Valley—"like the garden of the Lord." Remember that phrase "Lifted up his eyes." It connects significantly to the end of the story. Lot fixed his eyes on the sweetest territory anyone could see from that vantage point. There's not a hint of gratitude or deference in Lot. All he cares about is himself. But we know the rest of the story and it is hinted at here. All is not as it seems. There was a certain courage of faith in Abram that, no matter what Lot did, God would keep his promise to Abram concerning the blessing of the Promised Land.

Just about everyone knows what happened to Lot. He chose the Jordan Valley. He went east—a direction away from the Lord and his blessing in Genesis. He and his uncle separated. Abram went to the land of Canaan—God's plan all along. Lot settled near Sodom (v. 12). Is there anybody who hasn't heard of Sodom and Gomorrah? Verse 13 says it all: "Now the men of Sodom were wicked, great sinners against the LORD." Talk about a setup for disaster just a short distance down the road (Gen. 19). Why? It was all because Lot's eyes were lifted up on the things of this world and not on the things of the Lord (1 John 2:15–17). John Calvin warned:

> Our eyes are not to be trusted; but that we must rather be on our guard lest we be ensnared by them, and be encircled, unawares, with many evils; just as Lot, when he fancied that he was dwelling in paradise, was nearly plunged into the depths of hell.[10]

6. Trusting God to Keep Promises

They parted. Lot went in his direction; Abram took off in his. But the relationship was intact. There was no breach, in large part due to Abram's magnanimous spirit. And notice what happens next: God comes to Abram (v. 14)! At the point where he magnanimously released and surrendered, the Lord shows up saying, "Lift up your eyes." The writer wants us to make the connection with his previous use of that phrase (v. 10). Because Abram fixed his eyes in faith on God, he got rewarded with a look in all four directions at the land that would belong to him (v. 14). Nothing was lost by his generosity. Everything was assured. Abram's confidence in God's faithfulness to keep his promises freed him to practice magnanimous generosity. This *Tabletalk* devotional got it right:

> Such willingness displays great confidence in the Lord's promise, as well as great faithfulness to act in the same way God did toward him— graciously. Abram's offer was possible because he was confident God would indeed give him a good land, even if he had to give up the portion of it that seemed the best. And in putting another before him for the sake of peace, Abram was already displaying the work of the Spirit in his heart, for it is the peacemaker who shall inherit the earth (Matt. 5:9).[11]

Honestly, these last three aspects of magnanimity hit pretty close to home in my own life and ministry lately. I turned sixty-five a few months back. Welcome to the world of Medicare and AARP membership. As the old saying goes, I ain't getting any younger! Before long I will need to pass the pastoral baton to a younger pastor to carry on the ministry at OGC. Let me be clear: I've committed from the outset that nothing matters more to me than contributing to a peaceful pastoral succession process from number three to four in our church's history. But here's the rub: I can't retire. I'm not positioned financially to do so. I will have to work to provide for my wife Jan and our future. But I have no idea, at this writing, what God has for me in terms of my next vocational calling. Frankly, the whole deal scares me. I'm tempted to hang on to my role at Orlando Grace to keep paying the bills. More and more pastors these financially challenging days are doing just that.

But I keep asking myself, *What's the loving thing to do for OGC?* Now, I don't want to pull the rip cord too late on my stewardship here for sure, but I also don't want to bolt too soon either. I refuse to leave the church in the lurch if I can possibly avoid doing so. According to the Vanderbloemen Search Group, a search firm specifically focused on connecting churches and ministries with the right leadership for their teams, messy transitions occur in as many as one out of four situations.[12] Some of the case study examples of succession failure cited in the research sober me, especially for a church with a checkered leadership transition history like ours.

So what does all this mean? I've initiated the conversation about succession. I'm driving this train down the track. I don't want my elders in the awkward place of having to force the issue with me and the conflict that it might create. I want them to be able, with no hindrance from me, to get on with leading the church, which will remain in their charge long after I'm history. We've studied William Vanderbloemen and Warren Bird's book about church succession, *Next*, in depth. Four of us recently attended a Lifeway Conference in Nashville on succession at every level of ministry, including the role of lead pastor.

Inevitably, all that research and the conversation it engendered led to the inevitable. We had to land on an end date. *Gulp.* Theory must become reality. I knew as soon as we would nail down a hard-target, end-of-the-road, see-ya-later-PC deadline for my last Sunday service, it would galvanize a series of actions in a way that mere discussion would never do. Earlier this week, at this writing (December 2017), I agreed to Fall 2019 as the timetable for my exit—without knowing, as of yet, where God wants me to go from here. But I am absolutely certain, for the sake of the peace of OGC and the preservation of her unity, I must release control, courageously accept outcomes, and trust God for a boatload of promises about my household's future, otherwise forget about putting this book out in the marketplace. Why am I not surprised that the Lord would choose to test me on the very principles I deem necessary to teach through *The Peacemaking Church*?

Now, you might be thinking, *I could never do what Abram did in his circumstance or what you did in yours, especially if money was at stake.* Left to yourself, I would agree—you can't. Nor can I. But think about a New Testament occasion for generosity at the church of Corinth for a moment. Paul seeks to motivate a generous, magnanimous spirit on the part of the Corinthians to contribute to the offering for the Jerusalem church in need (2 Cor. 8–9). How does he do it? "For you know the grace of our Lord Jesus Christ, that though he was rich, yet for your sake he became poor, so that you by his poverty might become rich" (2 Cor. 8:9). Just as Abram, the superior, humbled himself with magnanimous generosity before inferior Lot to preserve peace, thus showing himself the spiritual superior, so Jesus, our superior in every way, humbled himself before our inferior, sinful selves on the cross. As a result, we were enriched and he was exalted by the Father with the name above all names (Phil. 2:5–11).

Trust in Jesus, Abram's greater son (Matt. 1:1), can transform our hearts from petty selfishness to magnanimous generosity. That alone enables us to embrace the peacemaking ways modeled by Abram. Lift up your eyes to him (Heb. 12:1–2). And the next time you sense a relational disaster in the making, determine to intercept it before it happens. How can you help ensure you rarely, if ever, have to worry about that with your church leaders? That question leads us to another practice we must master for fostering unity.

9

Honoring Spiritual Leaders for Their Exceptional Work

Love one another with brotherly affection. Outdo one another in showing honor.

Romans 12:10

We can all learn to follow imperfect leaders. We have no other choice, for there is no perfect leader in a fallen world, and as followers, this is what we are called to do.

Tara Klena Barthel and David V. Edling[1]

Sunday, August 24, 1662, witnessed a great turning point in English Christianity. Dubbed "the Great Ejection," some two thousand ministers left the national church for reasons of conscience. That "Farewell Sunday," Puritan giants such as Richard Baxter, Thomas Manton, Thomas Watson, and numerous others delivered parting sermons to their congregations.[2] Thomas Brooks prepared his own but apparently never got to preach it. Consequently, he preserved his in written form. His conclusion consisted of twenty-seven "legacies" he wished to impart to his people. The tenth revealed his passion for the church to excel in preserving unity:

Labour mightily for a healing spirit. This legacy I would leave with you as a matter of great concernment. To repeat: *Labour mightily for a healing spirit.* Away with all discriminating names whatever that may hinder the applying of balm to heal your wounds. Labour for a healing spirit. Discord and division become no Christian. For wolves to worry the lambs, is no wonder; but for one lamb to worry another, this is unnatural and monstrous. God hath made his wrath to smoke against us for the divisions and heart-burnings that have been amongst us. Labour for a oneness in love and affection with every one that is one with Christ. Let their forms be what they will, that which wins most upon Christ's heart, should win most upon ours, and that is his own grace and holiness. The question should be, What of the Father, what of the Son, what of the Spirit shines in this or that person? And accordingly let your love and your affections run out.[3]

In his first letter to a mostly healthy church at Thessalonica, the apostle Paul issued a variety of exhortations. One in particular championed Brooks's legacy of laboring mightily for a healing spirit. "Be at peace among yourselves" (1 Thess. 5:13). The verb is an imperative. He commands this. It is not optional to pursue peace in the body of Christ—and get this—*constantly*, no less. He uses the present tense. It conveys a continuous kind of action. An alternate translation could rightly read, "Keep on being at peace among yourselves."

Hebrews 12:14 slants it this way: "Strive for peace with everyone." Paul pressed, as noted before, "If possible, so far as it depends on you, live peaceably with all" (Rom. 12:18). Brooks nailed it. "Labour *mightily* for a healing spirit." Do-your-best preservers of congregational unity should bring a lot of energy to peacemaking in the church. It will always rank high in their priorities as members of a fellowship.

In 1 Thessalonians 5:12–13, Paul zeroes in on relationships between the people and their leaders. He spells out a practice they must master, if they are to excel as a peacemaking people. Concluding with some final instructions, he writes:

> We ask you, brothers, to respect those who labor among you and are over you in the Lord and admonish you, and to esteem them very highly in love because of their work. Be at peace among yourselves.

The apostle targets principally the followers—the greater majority of any congregation. The principle for laboring mightily to safeguard unity in this case is this: peacemaking people in Christ's church treat their officers with utmost honor given the nature of their work.

Paul models a peacemaking spirit himself in carefully chosen words up front. "We *ask* you, brothers" (v. 12, emphasis added). He commands at the end of verse 13, but he leads with a request. The same word *ask* appears earlier in the letter coupled with another term: "We ask and urge you" (4:1). The two verbs combine to reveal his heart. He pleads with them. He appeals to their familial sentiments—like a father would his children. With respect to their attitude toward their leaders, elders and deacons alike, he implores them for a particular spirit.

The What—Respect and Esteem

Paul uses two infinitives synonymously to drive home his point. "To respect" (5:12) and "to esteem" (v. 13). The former is the Greek word "to know." The text could read, "We ask you, brothers, to know those who labor among you." He desires something more than raw recognition or mere dutiful honor. In other words, don't just acknowledge them because you must obey. Know them. Relate to them. Personally engage them. That fits well with the addition of the words "in love" that go with the second infinitive, "to esteem."

Of course, this assumes that church leaders consent to and pursue being known. There are several ways I seek to do this in my role as lead pastor at OGC. First, I hang around the auditorium after services whenever I can. I want to engage people. I encourage folks to come pray with me and the rest of our elders about their needs. I want to meet the guests. I don't bolt to my study or out the side door to escape connection with people. Sometimes it takes so long to work through the line that I end up shutting off the lights and locking the doors behind me. No problem.

Second, I teach most of the sessions of our twelve-week new member's class. I want to get to know new folks and I want them to get to know me. When I can't teach, I have other elders lead the class so our new people get the opportunity to connect with them as well. Jan joins me in each class. People need to get acquainted with her as well. A highlight of each of our two installments per year of "Discover OGC" is a luncheon we host at our house on a Sunday after church. There is something about bridging relational gaps between leaders and followers that is made so much easier when ministry occurs in the pastor's home. Whenever Jan and I do pastoral care together, we schedule meetings as often as possible at our home as opposed to in my study.

Third, Jan and I attend one of our community groups. It has worked out well that I don't have to lead a group. I'm just another participant. It takes place in someone else's home. I get to connect with folks in that environment just like everybody else. This is huge. People get to know one another, including their pastors, in a small group context much more effectively than they possibly can in the average large group Sunday morning setting.

Four, I try to be vulnerable. I admit my failures, even publicly when necessary. That mess I nearly made that I confessed way back in the introduction? I mentioned it at an appropriate place in a sermon a few weeks later. I didn't go into detail. I told folks not to ask me any questions about it. Case closed. However, they got a glimpse as to just how flawed a vessel serves their interests at OGC to this very day. Believe me, vulnerability breeds approachability. If the people think you're some kind of super-spiritual rock star with whom they can't identify, they won't gravitate toward you; they will keep their distance. Exercise care here. There are risks. Be discreet. Don't manipulate. Just be flat-out honest.

Writing this chapter prompted a question in me. *Who in my own life and ministry, other than my bride, excels in making me feel respected and encouraged?* I immediately thought of a woman in our church. In recent years, Lucy (not her real name) has gone out of her way nearly every Sunday to thank me for a message, appreciate some aspect of our ministry, and overall cheerlead for my work. Interestingly enough, that has not always been the case. I recall a difficult meeting we had several years ago with her, her husband, and another one of our elders. She engaged that afternoon with a multipage document listing her concerns about me, my preaching, and personal ministry. The interview lasted a couple of hours. I remember it being pretty painful. I can tend to take criticism personally. It was a bit like having a root canal without the benefit of a nerve block.

Frankly, I don't remember how that conversation ended. Thankfully, she and her husband remained in the church—as faithful a couple as you will find. This chapter got me wondering what changed. So I called up some courage and decided to ask her one Sunday after a service. I told her about how I was working on the content of 1 Thessalonians 5. I thanked her for how I regarded her as a singularly exceptional example of the peacemaking values of respect and esteem for me as a pastor. She smiled when I ventured to remember with her about friction-filled days gone by. "What changed?" I asked—careful to assure her that I wasn't fishing for affirmation over ways I tweaked things since that talk, though I did. She had made some excellent points.

With remarkable ease, Lucy listed the ways God had worked to turn the tide. The first thing she said was, "You listened that day. You sat through those thousands of pages (her hyperbole was showing) without interrupting. I thought that had to have been difficult for you." My mind immediately went to Ephesians 4:2–3 and the virtues necessary to preserve unity. I'm so grateful God gave me grace to act with a measure of humility and patience in that conversation. I have no explanation for responding the way I did other than gospel mercy.

What she said next resonated powerfully for me on the importance of knowing and being known as a leader. Lucy cited the way I endured suffering from 2014 through 2017. The loss of my first son and wife, the disintegration of my jaw from cancer treatment back in 2005, and the marathon surgeries required to reconstruct it preached a sermon of life humbled under the mighty hand of God (1 Pet. 5:6–7) in ways no number of regular Sunday messages could do. Now, again, I take no credit for any of that. I plead only the all-sufficient grace of God where his power was made perfect in weakness (2 Cor. 12:9–10). This exchange made me so glad that I steered through those suffering waters pretty much as an open book for our people. In Lucy's case, she felt she knew me in a more thorough way. It translated into respect for me. I praise God that she shared with me how the Lord helped her grow as a 1 Thessalonians 5:12–13 peacemaker.

As if all that wasn't more than enough, Lucy wrote these additional words about another contributing factor to her journey of increasingly embracing me with respect as a pastor in her life:

> My husband often reminded me of how Curt was a great encourager to him and how skillfully Curt led small men's groups. My husband grew a lot and enjoyed those groups very much. I was grateful to Curt for that and thus knew I had to hang in there with him, as our pastor. A few years after my long, difficult conversation

with Curt, we had a shocking and horrible time of extended family troubles. Curt was faithfully there for us as we endured this season. His unfailing pastoral wisdom and counsel, plus his prayerful and emotional support, were invaluable. Naturally my appreciation for him as our pastor grew tremendously and more than made up for the previous negativity I had felt and expressed toward him.

I have to admit—I'm a bit reluctant to include this in the story. It feels self-aggrandizing to me. It doesn't mesh with Ephesians 4:2 humility. I don't mean to toot my own horn. Forgive me if I have overstepped my bounds, reader friend. These words came unsolicited as a result of pursuing informed consent from Lucy to share her story. She blew me away. I, like a zillion other pastors of all sized churches, just want to check the "faithful" box on his CV at the end of his tour (1 Cor. 4:2). All I can say/plead/beg/pray for shepherds and sheep alike is this: *don't give up on one another!* Hang in there. The peace and purity of your church is worth the blood, sweat, and tears of long-suffering together. Phew! Okay, back to the Thessalonians.

The word *esteem* normally gets translated "to consider" or "to think" in a certain way. Here the context dictates a nuance of honor. We are to think of our leaders in terms of esteem—and to no small degree, for that matter! "Esteem them *very highly* in love" (1 Thess. 5:13, emphasis added). One commentator calls "very highly" a "triple Pauline intensive."[4] It means "quite beyond all measure." It conveys the highest form of comparison imaginable. This construction appears rarely in the New Testament but perhaps most vividly in another of Paul's letters. "Now to him who is able to do *far more abundantly* than all we ask or think" (Eph. 3:20, emphasis added).

Tara Barthel relates a story about a woman she once helped that illustrates the kind of spirit Paul advocates in these verses:

> Her marriage was very difficult, and her church leaders, though involved, were inexperienced in biblical counseling and biblical peacemaking. They made mistakes but they truly wanted to do what was biblically correct. Although this woman suffered greatly, she did so with great love and patience, realizing that her temporary circumstance was not just about her—it was also about helping her church leaders grow in knowledge, wisdom, and ability to serve as officers of Christ's church. . . . This dear woman remembered that leaders are human; leaders are in the process of growing too. They are just as much in need of grace as followers are.[5]

The Why—Because of Their Work

So far we have answered the "what" question from this passage. Followers who master peacemaking with leaders in their church treat them with the utmost relational, loving esteem/honor/respect possible. Now we are ready to ask the "why" question. The answer comes in the middle of verse 13—"because of their work."

I make it a point most every Sunday before the worship service to eyeball the congregation, looking for new people. If possible, I head their way to welcome them. One Sunday I approached a lady who was visiting for the first time. I introduced myself by my first name. She smiled and replied, "Hi, Curt." She shook my hand. But then she paused, maybe catching a glimpse of my name tag, and actually gasped a bit. "Are you the pastor?" she asked. "Well, yes, I am," I answered. And then she apologized. She explained, "Then I should have addressed you as 'pastor.'"

I assured her that she did not offend me. Lots of folks around Orlando Grace call me "PC" for short. I actually like the affection behind the nickname! Some even address me by my first name, without the title. It really makes no difference to me. But the fact that she took the office seriously and wanted to convey that even by the way she addressed me made me think. She gets this verse. Don't get me wrong. This principle for safeguarding unity isn't necessarily about titles. But particularly in a conflict involving your shepherds, if peacemaking and Paul's teaching matter here, you will want to take enormous pains with the way you go about communicating. You will govern your tone of voice, choice of words, and overall demeanor so that you guard your heart from disrespect.

Paul lists four aspects of the officers' work that necessitate honoring them as an essential part of pursuing peace and preserving unity in Christ's church. Let's look at them each in turn and make some practical applications.

1. Family Work

Remember how Paul begins? "We ask you" (1 Thess. 5:12). He urges gently; he doesn't pull apostolic rank. And he writes with affection, calling them "brothers." Of course, as the ESV marginal note clarifies, he means "brothers and sisters"—both men and women. He builds everything he commends here on the gospel foundation of brotherhood. We are family. Before we are elders, deacons, or congregants, we are brothers and sisters in Christ. The church is God's family. What should distinguish us above all else is the love we have for one another. This should be our relentless rally cry: "Love one another with brotherly affection. Outdo one another in showing honor" (Rom. 12:10). For followers, that must be especially true of the way they esteem their church officers. When you engage an officer about some issue in the church, picture him with his family hat on—your brother—before his leader hat.

One Sunday morning, a number of years ago, I went on an ill-advised tirade during the announcement segment of the worship service. A new round of what we call Equipping Hour (think Sunday school) classes lay before us. Attendance at these often started strong but waned as weeks went by. In an effort to motivate greater participation, I went on a legalistic rant and rave. I mean, it was ugly. It was so bad my wife Nancy actually pulled me aside during the music to express her dismay at my meltdown!

If that wasn't bad enough, a week or so later our pastoral intern asked to meet me for lunch. After the usual chitchat, the young man courageously confronted that Sunday's mess-up. I'll never forget what he said. "Pastor Curt, the only thing that entire day that pointed me to the gospel was the baptisms at the end." This clearly had not been my finest pastoral hour. That both my wife and an intern needed to exhort me about it humbled me big-time. I got the message. I determined never to do that again. Both the way Nancy and our intern approached me made all the difference in the world in the way I reacted. They never lost sight of respect for my calling and authority as an elder. They entreated me with esteeming love as a brother—and in my wife's case, also as her husband!

2. Hard Work

See the word *labor* in verse 12? The Greek language has a variety of terms for work. Paul uses here a verb form of a particularly vivid word. It describes toil, labor, or work so depleting it leaves one weary—completely exhausted. The root of the word means "beaten," as in this kind of work leaves you feeling like you just went fifteen rounds with Muhammad Ali. Paul uses the same word when he speaks of those "who labor in preaching and teaching" (1 Tim. 5:17), a principal role of an elder. In his own testimony, Paul claimed: "I worked harder than any of them, though it was not I, but the grace of God that is with me" (1 Cor. 15:10).

If church leaders are worth their salt, I guarantee you they know the reality of hard work. They've lost sleep, sacrificed family time, and put their own needs second to those they serve countless times. And sometimes it just leaves a servant feeling spent. Not only that, but by Jesus's own admission the laborers are few (Matt. 9:37). So they are likely undermanned on their team for the tasks on their list. These realities of church ministry alone are reason enough, Paul argues, for followers to pursue peace by treating their officers with respect.

In my role as a shepherd of God's people, I get called upon often to assist folks in resolving disputes. I find the effort, time, and commitments necessary for effective peacemaking among the toughest assignments in my ministry. One of my more recent experiences in that area involved a father and his adult daughter. They had become estranged over a serious matter in their family history. They could not even sit down at the same table to talk through the issues. Unable to resolve things on their own, they asked me for help.

I always approach these challenges the same way. First, I meet with the individuals alone for conflict coaching—multiple times if necessary. Then we meet for the actual mediation. Along the way I try to help identify issues, concerns, offenses, idols of the heart, and paths to reconciliation. It can be brutally exhausting work. The process with the father and daughter was easier than some but still took its toll. In the end they reconciled with a huge hug. They thanked me, of course. What I did not expect was to receive a note in the mail later that week from the wife and mother of the family. She thanked me profusely for my labors. She quoted her husband as saying, "I've got my daughter back!" Few things are more rewarding.

Over the years I have kept a file full of notes and cards like that. Hers joined the rest. I call it my "Why I Became a Pastor File." I pull it out on days I think about abandoning ship and becoming a Walmart greeter. Few things convey more honor and respect to someone like me in pastoral ministry than tangible appreciation. By the way, when is the last time you took a deacon or elder aside to thank them for their faithful service tending the finances or some other aspect of church life? How about writing your pastor a note this week appreciating their efforts in the pulpit or some other way they have ministered effectively to you? Trust me—it will make their day and you will be doing your part to promote peace in the church.

3. Leading Work

Part of what makes this kind of work hard is its leadership component. Paul writes, "Respect those who labor among you and *are over you* in the Lord" (1 Thess. 5:12, emphasis added). The verb *over* is made up of two Greek words, literally "to stand" and "before." It means to provide oversight. Paul exhorted the elders at Ephesus about this aspect of the work: "Pay careful attention to yourselves and to all the flock, in which the Holy Spirit has made you *overseers*, to care for the church of God" (Acts 20:28, emphasis added). These servants preside over the affairs of the congregation, keeping watch for its welfare and good order.

Please don't miss those words "in the Lord." The elder's domain is spiritual. It's the church. Elders tend to the affairs of Christ within the local congregation as his representatives doing his business. I love to start every new member class the same way. I introduce myself: Curt Heffelfinger. I give my title: I am the pastor-teacher here at OGC. Then I add, "I am not the senior pastor." Then I ask, "Would you like to know who is?" Inevitably I get a "Yes." Some just go ahead and blurt out the answer, "Jesus." Jesus is the chief Shepherd of his church (1 Pet. 5:4). Every elder and deacon is nothing more than Christ's underling/steward.

The writer to the Hebrews captures a sobering nuance to the leading work of church officers:

> Obey your leaders and submit to them, for they are keeping watch over your souls, as those who will have to give an account. Let them do this with joy and not with groaning, for that would be of no advantage to you. (Heb. 13:17)

By the way—to beat this drum one more time—you simply cannot obey this verse if you don't belong to a local church as a member, partner, or whatever you want to call it.[6] Someone in a local context of Jesus's universal church needs your informed consent to take responsibility for your spiritual welfare. Alfred Poirier notes this as one of several aspects of a biblical basis for covenant membership in a local church:

> The New Testament writers assume that Christians can identify their leaders to whom they have voluntarily submitted themselves. . . . And conversely, they expect the leaders of a church to be able to identify those members for whom they must give an account. . . . Yet God will not hold a pastor liable for failing to discharge his duties as shepherd over sheep that he cannot determine are his own.[7]

But my primary point here is that a lack of respect toward the officers for their work can tempt them to groan. It can tempt them to discouragement. Don't go there. Threatening Christ's servants' joy through disrespect and being unduly difficult to shepherd will not profit you and will jeopardize the peace of the church. Please determine to be easily led for the sake of the unity of your fellowship.

Here are some practical suggestions on this front. Are you going to be gone for several weeks and go missing on Sundays for vacation, business, or some other reason? Let your pastor know in advance so he does not wonder if you are okay. If he tries to reach you via text, email, or phone to check up on you, to ask for your help, or to follow up on something, don't make it hard for him. Be responsive, be prompt, be cooperative in every way you can. You will give him such joy. Of course, if you have not yet become a member of your church, determine to take advantage of the soonest possible opportunity you can to identify with that congregation and its leaders. Finally, if you are wondering about changing churches for some reason, please counsel with your leadership before that train has left the station. Don't make them have to track you down. When you get your pastor's "bless and release" (I try to do this whenever possible after making sure heart and/or conflict issues aren't going unaddressed) be diligent to transfer your membership as soon as possible so everyone knows who's responsible for whom.

We once had a newcomer come from another church in the area to make her home at Orlando Grace. Rarely have I witnessed greater peacemaking/preserving unity care in the way she navigated the process. At one point I got copied on an email she sent in advance of meeting with her leaders at her former church, wondering if I had any input to offer. Here's what she wrote:

Dear_____,

I know we haven't been able to nail down a time to meet yet, but I do appreciate the efforts and look forward to sitting down and talking soon. I have been thinking and praying more about how to move forward in a way that doesn't undermine you or the church, how much to say or not say to people. I wrote out some thoughts as a rough draft to a letter and thought maybe it would be good to let you look over it before we meet so that you can process and think through if it sounds okay and if you feel it is honoring to you. Maybe there are other thoughts you have, and perspective, as I think through all of the logistics moving forward. I really do mean what I wrote. I love you all very much and am very grateful for you. I have no regrets in getting to be a part of (name of church) for all of these years and am proud to share with others about the investment and impact you've all had in my life.

Wow. That content alone blew me away for its 1 Thessalonians 5:12–13 spirit from start to finish. But then I went on to read her draft message to the congregation:

Dear_____,

It has been so good to be home, to come to services lately and to get to see so many of you. I am so humbled and encouraged by your prayers and support and interest and love for me. For about a year or more I have been praying and thinking through a very difficult decision. I believe God is leading me on to a new church home. This is not a decision I make lightly and not one that I am making because I am at odds with anyone at our church.

I am extremely grateful for (names of key servants) for their huge investment in my life and for all of their sacrificial leadership. The church staff works so very hard pouring their lives into our lives and in laboring to see lost people come to Christ. They are men placed in authority, by God, to shepherd and watch over our souls. I am very grateful for their character and example. I am so thankful for the church staff's incredible patience with me over the years, letting me serve and make mistakes and learn. I am so very thankful for all of you and love you all very much. Thank you so much for your generosity and for your patience with me as well.

Over the past twelve years I have wrestled through a lot of questions, studying Scripture in figuring out owning my faith and convictions for myself. I have landed in a different place on some theological and philosophical issues as it pertains to ministry. I do not think this letter is the place to go into detail on these things, but I am happy to answer any questions you may have if you want to talk with me personally. I believe it is very important to uphold one's biblical responsibilities as a church member and to have an attitude of submission. Though we might inevitably agree to disagree on some of the convictions I have come to, I hope that we can still remain friends as brothers and sisters in Christ and cheer each other on in ministry, holding each other up in prayer.

I just want to reiterate my love, gratitude, prayers and respect for Pastor _____ and all of the church staff. I still care very much for these dear families and want to remain in fellowship with them. I do not want my moving my church membership to in any way communicate to you that I think ill of them, of the church, or of any of you. I look forward to still coming to services from time to time and staying connected with you all. I continue to need and covet your prayers and continue to pray for you all.

My reply to her read this way:

Thanks, too, for inviting me into your process. All I can say is that I wish more folks who leave churches for whatever the reasons would go to the lengths you are attempting with (name of church). This is so well written. It is an excellent example of the spirit of Ephesians 4:1–3 and 1 Thessalonians 5:12–13. I have no critique, only praise. Please know that I am praying for God's favor and timing in getting to have a conversation with these leaders.

Leaving a church family for a new home presents unique challenges for safeguarding a congregation's unity. I wish more folks went to the pains exemplified above when that kind of hard decision must occur for whatever reasons. I can tell you, leaders really appreciate it, given the demands of their work.

4. Corrective Work

The last of three verbs in 1 Thessalonians 5:12 describing the nature of a church officer's work is the word *admonish*. Literally it means "to put in mind." It has instruction and teaching overtones. But more is involved in that. We get some help from what follows: "And we urge you, brothers, admonish the idle" (v. 14). Admonishment is confrontational in a good sense. It addresses sinful behaviors like idleness to help others change and grow. Apparently, some of the Thessalonians, confused about the doctrine of the return of Christ and its implications (see 4:13–5:11), stopped working for their provision. Instead they were waiting around for Jesus to come back. Paul urged that this kind of thing not go on unchecked.

Here is another example: "As for a person who stirs up division, after warning him once and then twice, have nothing more to do with him" (Titus 3:10). It is the job of elders to identify ungodly behavior in followers of Jesus—like divisiveness—and to help uproot the idols that lie beneath those sins. That, by the way, is terribly hard work. In some ways, I would say it's one of the hardest parts of a pastor's responsibilities. But it is absolutely essential ministry for the welfare of the flock. David Mathis, writing for *Desiring God*, explains why this kind of spiritual work by leaders, or anyone in our lives for that matter, deserves our utmost respect:

> How is it that God's reproof most often comes to us? Answer: in reproof from a brother or sister in Christ. We'll beware resisting the reproof of a fellow in Jesus, especially when it's echoed in multiple voices, knowing that likely we would be resisting the very reproof of God. When a brother or sister in Christ goes to the inconvenience to have the unpleasant conversation bringing correction into our lives, we should be floored with thanksgiving. . . . Count it as love from your brother, and as God's channel of his love for you.[8]

Here is another practical suggestion. Watch your attitude when a church officer attempts in love to take you aside to reprove or exhort you. You may not end up agreeing in the long run, but that is still such an important work for your spiritual well-being. Take it to heart. At least pray about it. Thank them for reaching out to you. Respect the fact that they went out of their way to risk speaking to you with truth in love (Eph. 4:15).

Earlier in this chapter I told the story of my all-star encourager, Lucy, and the challenging chat we had years before. She reminded me at the conclusion of our reminiscing that, after all my listening that day, I had offered her one thought of admonition to try and help her. I mentioned to her that Nancy and I had talked at one point about her tending toward being self-absorbed—that it made it challenging for others to engage her. Turns out she later went to my wife to ask for help in that area. I didn't remember that. She praised Nancy for her sweetness and the input she got from her. Not everyone will respond to correction as well as Lucy did. But we pastors must still do the hard work of admonishment just the same. Do you honor your spiritual leaders for their courage to confront in love in spite of their fears? The Bible says we should.

For all these reasons, followers should pursue peace by holding their leaders in the highest regard worthy of all esteem. This kind of honoring, submissive virtue does not come naturally. It is not our default heart setting as self-centered beings. I think that's why Paul motivates the way he does just before this context:

> For God has not destined us for wrath, but to obtain salvation through our Lord Jesus Christ, who died for us so that whether we are awake or asleep we might live with him. Therefore encourage one another and build one another up, just as you are doing. (1 Thess. 5:9–11)

To encourage one another, to build one another up, to honor one another, whether officers or not—these capacities come from him who died for us so that, whether we are awake or asleep, we might live with him. Tara Barthel and David Edling point to this kind of gospel motivation in lobbying for thinking the world of our church leaders:

> As you consider your role as a follower in your church . . . how are you affirming the gifts and strengths of your leaders, and how are you bearing with their weaknesses? Remember how gentle and patient God is toward you—that it is his kindness that "leads you toward repentance" (Rom. 2:4). . . . One of the most appreciative and encouraging things you can do for your leaders is to pray for them and let them know you are doing so. This will demonstrate your proactive devotion.[9]

Great concept, proactive devotion—and yet another practice contributing significantly to some very sweet rewards accompanying unity in the church, which is the high note on which the epilogue of *The Peacemaking Church* concludes.

141

Epilogue

Savoring the Pleasures That Accompany Unity

Behold, how good and pleasant it is when brothers dwell in unity!

Psalm 133:1

Blessed are the peacemakers, for they shall be called sons of God.

Matthew 5:9

When unity was broken, [Paul's] heart broke with it. When unity was strengthened his soul sang.

Paul Rees[1]

As I mentioned in chapter 7, I remarried relatively soon after losing my first wife, Nancy. God had brought Jan into our church three years before. Her first Sunday was the day after my son, Joshua, died at age thirty-five from heart failure. Little did anyone know that God in his kindness was preparing a second life partner for me. Who gets the blessing of uniting with one rock-star godly woman, let alone two in a lifetime?

Three months passed after our wedding before Jan and I spent our first extended weekend apart. She went to visit her daughter and family in another state. I stayed home to attend to my pastoral responsibilities.

Going about the house in her absence, it wasn't long before I delighted to discover notes she had hidden for me all over the place before she left town. I collected some sixteen of them. She placed them in the bathroom, on a clothes hook, in my chest of drawers, on the bed, in my desk, in the dishwasher and the dryer, even on the flower watering can! Every time I found one I could not help but laugh. Few things compare with the sweetness of a marriage where oneness shows itself in such tangible expressions of love.

The same can be said of churches that experience the blessing of unity. When followers of Jesus embrace the priorities that preserve unity, avoid the pitfalls that threaten unity, and master the practices that foster unity, they can expect to reap rewards and savor pleasures reserved for their excellence in guarding oneness in the church. In this epilogue, I want to encourage you to expect two blessings, beginning with a song to sing.

Have you ever stopped to think about the kind of things songwriters use as themes for their creations and artists tend to sing about? *US News* published an article on that very subject. It was based on a study conducted by North Carolina State University. Researchers used a data-mining program to comb the lyrics of the songs that reached No. 1 on Billboard's Hot 100 list between 1960 and 2009—nearly one thousand songs in all. Twelve themes ran through the fifty-year span of music: loss, desire, aspiration, breakup, pain, inspiration, nostalgia, rebellion, being jaded, desperation, escapism, and confusion—most songs with those themes were emotional in tone.[2]

We sing about a lot of themes in our culture, some surprising, some not. Apparently, we do not often focus on the theme of unity. Its opposite, "breakup," runs through song lyrics, but getting along well with others does not. The Scriptures, however, do sing about the sweetness of unity in God's hymnbook.

A Song of Ascents. Of David.

> Behold, how good and pleasant it is
>   when brothers dwell in unity!
> It is like the precious oil on the head,
>   running down on the beard,
> on the beard of Aaron,
>   running down on the collar of his robes!

It is like the dew of Hermon,
  which falls on the mountains of Zion!
For there the LORD has commanded the blessing,
  life forevermore. (Ps. 133:1–3)

The inscription that precedes this three-verse poem informs the reader that it is indeed a song, but a particular kind of song within the Psalter—a "Song of Ascents." It falls within a series of songs by the same title, Psalms 120 to 134. These were tunes likely sung by all Israelite pilgrims as they would make their way up to Jerusalem to worship at the temple during various feasts.

There's no missing the theme of this one: "Behold, how good and pleasant it is when brothers dwell in unity!" (v. 1). The word translated "dwell" has the idea of permanence, consistency, an ongoing reality behind it. The inscription attributes authorship to King David. But it doesn't tell us anything about the circumstances. A lot of scholars think he penned it during the events of 2 Samuel 5, when all Israel gathered for his coronation as king over united Israel. That memorable event followed the horrible disunity, enmity, and warfare with the house of King Saul. That would fit, but no one can say for certain. Regardless, when members of every Israelite tribe would make the trek to Zion to unite in corporate worship in the temple, singing Psalm 133 along the way would remind them of the sweet blessing of coming together for a common purpose with great joy.

The big takeaway from the psalm is this: unity among God's people over time is very much worth praising the Lord for in worshipful singing. A lot of themes make sense for worship songwriting. The blessing of unity should rank near the top of the list for two reasons according to King David—its sweetness and its source.

The song starts with an exclamation. "Behold!" It's like David stares at this deal and grabs us by the back of the neck to fix our gaze on the stunning reality that it is. Everything about this opening line conveys David's wonder and admiration at the very special, perhaps even rare and exceptional, nature of things when God's people actually get along well with one another over time.

He calls it both "good" and "pleasant." The word translated "good" is the same word used throughout Genesis 1 in the creation account. It is the more objective word of the two in the psalm. It pronounces the moral worth of unity. "Pleasant" is variously translated as "delightful," "lovely," and "sweet." It is the more subjective word of the two. We find it in 2 Samuel 1:23 to describe the best-of-friends relationship enjoyed by David and Jonathan. The great Baptist preacher of nineteenth-century England, Charles Spurgeon, got the significance of the pairing:

> The combination of the two adjectives "good" and "pleasant" is more remarkable than the conjunction of two stars of the first magnitude: for a thing to be "good" is good, but for it also to be pleasant is better. All men love pleasant things, and yet it frequently happens that the pleasure is evil; but here the condition is as good as it is pleasant, as pleasant as it is good, for the same "how" is set before each qualifying word.[3]

Spurgeon did his homework. The Hebrew text does in fact repeat the word "how" before each adjective. It could well read, "How good and how pleasant it is," which makes the sense even more emphatic.

David now proceeds to paint a word picture to describe just how good, pleasant, and sweet a thing it really is when God's people get along over time. "It is like the precious oil on the head, running down on the beard, on the beard of Aaron, running down on the collar of his robes" (Ps. 133:2). We find background for making sense of this figure of speech in the law:

> The Lord said to Moses, "Take the finest spices: of liquid myrrh 500 shekels, and of sweet-smelling cinnamon half as much, that is, 250, and 250 of aromatic cane, and 500 of cassia, according to the shekel of the sanctuary, and a hin of olive oil. And you shall make of these a sacred anointing oil blended as by the perfumer; it shall be a holy anointing oil. With it you shall anoint the tent of meeting and the ark of the testimony, and the table and all its utensils, and the lampstand and its utensils, and the altar of incense, and the altar of burnt offering with all its utensils and the basin and its stand. You shall consecrate them, that they may be most holy. Whatever touches them will become holy. You shall anoint Aaron and his sons, and consecrate them, that they may serve me as priests. And you shall say to the people of Israel, 'This shall be my holy anointing oil throughout your generations. It shall not be poured on the body of an ordinary person, and you shall make no other like it in composition. It is holy, and it shall be holy to you.'" (Exod. 30:22–32)

146

Lots of things combine in the oil/priest figure to illustrate the extraordinary preciousness of unity in the body of Christ. There are multiple fine spices at great cost. There is a sweet-smelling, perfumelike fragrance. There is a copious amount used. Note the path of the oil in anointing: from head, to beard, and finally to collar. All parts are affected, from top to bottom. Everybody profits when unity exists. Most importantly, there is a setting-apart for sacred purposes. What role did Aaron as the high priest, and every other priest after him, fulfill on behalf of God's people? Mediator! They performed the animal sacrifices and offerings that would secure the people's forgiveness from sin and assurance of peace with God. What could be sweeter, more priceless, better than that?

So we should sing unity's song with great emotion in worshipful praise for its exquisite sweetness on so many levels. But the king suggests a second reason. Here comes simile number two. "It is like the dew of Hermon, which falls on the mountains of Zion!" (Ps. 133:3). The first word picture likened our unity to priests and their oil. It emphasized its sweetness. This second word picture likens our getting along to mountains, particularly Zion, and their dew. It emphasizes the ultimate source of all unity among God's people: God himself.

Once again, we have to wrestle with a cultural and geographical phenomenon that would have made a great deal of sense to David's audience but leaves us scratching our heads. In arid Palestine little to no rain falls from April to October. If it were not for the tremendous amounts of moisture from dew that accumulated each morning due to the geographical and atmospheric conditions of the region, vegetation would perish, crops would fail, and great hardship would result. The *International Standard Bible Encyclopedia* notes the unique benefit derived from Mt. Hermon, to the north of Jerusalem:

> Mt. Hermon is the source of many blessings to the land over which it so proudly lifts its splendid form. Refreshing breezes blow from its cold heights. Its snows are carried to Damascus and to the towns on the seaboard, where, mingled with the sharab, "drink," they mitigate the heat of the Syrian summer. Great reservoirs in the depths of the mountain, fed by the melting snows, find outlet in the magnificent springs at Chasbeiyeh, Tell el-Kady, and Banias, while the dew-clouds of Hermon bring a benediction wherever they are carried (Ps. 133:3).[4]

Zion's hills, while not to the same extent as Hermon, enjoyed a similar blessing upon which so much of life depended.

Now, here's the point. Dew was regarded as a singular symbol of God's blessing, especially along with rain, for these very benefits. This was so true that the Lord directly compares himself to it: "I will be like the dew to Israel" (Hos. 14:5). He sends it (Mic. 5:7). He withholds it (1 Kings 17:1). Like the dew, so is our unity. The rest of Psalm 133:3 declares, "for there the LORD has commanded the blessing, life forevermore." "Command" and "send" are synonymous in this context. Getting along over time comes to God's people from him. It's a gift. He is its ultimate source.

The structure and flow of this psalm further emphasize this idea of God as the source of unity for which we should give him such exuberant, song-filled praise. In verse 2, David repeats the words "running down." In verse 3, he used the word "falls." All three are the same Hebrew word. Unity in the church flows from the top down—from God to us. We don't create it; he gifts it to us. We are called to preserve it eagerly, but if we possess it to maintain it, that is only because he blessed us with it in the first place. Alexander Strauch is right: "God is the source of *shalom*, and his peace is to be one of the great blessings his people enjoy."[5]

The irony of all this is that David, who wrote this psalm enamored with the sweetness and source of unity among his people, eventually destroyed it for his own household. There came the fateful day in 2 Samuel 11 when he stayed home from war, eyed bathing-beauty Bathsheba from the palace rooftop, and sinned greatly with her. The next chapter records the consequences that shattered his family oneness from that day forward: "Now therefore the sword shall never depart from your house, because you have despised me and have taken the wife of Uriah the Hittite to be your wife" (2 Sam. 12:10).

Centuries later, David's greater Son, King Jesus, a priest better than Aaron, came to the very same hill called Zion and its city, known as Jerusalem, to offer his perfectly righteous life on the cross. There he purchased forgiveness before God Most Holy for David's and every other elect person's sin. He won back the peace sin robs from us all. Thus Paul declared: "For he himself is our peace" (Eph. 2:14). As a result, we now belong to a kingdom place even better than earthly Jerusalem with superior reason to sing—the ultimate blessing of life forevermore described vividly by the writer to the Hebrews:

> But you have come to Mount Zion and to the city of the living God, the heavenly Jerusalem, and to innumerable angels in festal gathering, and to the assembly of the firstborn who are enrolled in heaven, and to God, the judge of all, and to the spirits of the righteous made perfect, and to Jesus, the mediator of a new covenant, and to the sprinkled blood that speaks a better word than the blood of Abel. (Heb. 12:22–24)

Here are some practical takeaways to keep in mind from "Unity's Song." Make a habit of praising God with singing for the gift of unity. A psalter provides a convenient way to sing the psalms in both private and corporate worship.[6] Unfortunately, not many worship songs these days focus on this crucial theme of unity.[7] Perhaps more Christian song-writers will take up the challenge in the future. I certainly hope so!

Prize unity for the exceedingly sweet and good gift from God that it is. Regard it as supremely valuable. While thanking God for it, pray often that your church might continue to enjoy it. Don't take it for granted. Entreat the Lord for his ongoing blessing. Pastors, let us model this by often praying for the peace and unity of our churches in prayer meetings and as part of our pastoral prayers during worship service.

This next application is so important. I beg you to receive it with every ounce of your being. Reject, hate, despise, deplore, and abhor—as God does—strife and discord among the brethren (Prov. 6:16–19). Put to death relentlessly the deeds of the flesh that can so easily and thoroughly disrupt peace. These include things like gossip, pride, selfishness, slander, backbiting, nosiness, adultery, and a host of other sins (Col. 3:5–11). Unity is an exceedingly fragile thing. It doesn't take much to jeopardize it. Embrace for all you're worth, with Jesus's supernatural help, the call to excel at safeguarding unity in the church, the challenge espoused throughout *The Peacemaking Church*.

Dr. Ligon Duncan, chancellor of Reformed Theological Seminary, once preached on Psalm 133 when he served as pastor of a congregation. He introduced his message this way:

Psalm 133 has been sung at Presbyterian General Assembly for probably close to five hundred years now and if you've ever been to a Presbyterian General Assembly you'll know why it needs to be sung there because unity is not something that Presbyterians are known for at their General Assembly. It used to be said that if the Scots couldn't find somebody to fight they'd fight one another and that national characteristic has apparently followed Presbyterians historically over the decades and centuries. But perhaps in faith and as an ideal, typically our General Assembly closes every year . . . with the singing of this psalm in a metrical version, an aspiration that we all have in our family.[8]

Presbyterians do not possess a corner on the market of problems with disunity. They plague churchgoers of every stripe. Eugene Peterson summarized the challenge before us:

Living together in a way that evokes the glad song of Psalm 133 is one of the great and arduous tasks before Christ's people. Nothing requires more attention and energy. It is easier to do almost anything else.[9]

Perhaps so, but it is also worth every bit of eager excellence we bring to the task. Would that we all would aspire in faith to the same ideal for the sake of the One who prayed that we might all be one as he and the Father are one (John 17:11).

I promised two blessings for champions of unity at the outset of this epilogue. In addition to a sweet song to sing, there is a coveted label to treasure. Jesus included it at the very beginning of his famous Sermon on the Mount in what we commonly refer to as "The Beatitudes" (Matt. 5:3–11). The word for "blessed" comes first in each verse for emphasis. That, along with the ninefold repetition of it in bullet-point fashion, makes it hard to miss the point. Jesus really wants to drive these ideas home to the hearts of his listeners on the mountainside in terms of how enviable a status each represents.

When my first wife's father passed away a number of years ago, I was privileged to deliver the eulogy at his memorial service. I loved the man. Throughout the eulogy I referred to him as "fortunate." I could easily have said "blessed." I wanted to convey something of the idea of how much blessing God had bestowed upon him. The rest of the tribute went on to describe the many ways.

Each of Jesus's Beatitudes details his prescription for a truly blessed life as possessors of the kingdom of God. Both verse 3 and verse 10 hold out this amazing possibility with the pronouncement, "theirs is the kingdom of heaven." Anyone who manifests these countercultural, otherworldly, supernaturally wrought characteristics of spiritual salvation in their everyday lives enjoys all kinds of enviable blessing.

Along with the assurance of the present possession of the kingdom of heaven come numerous future promises. Those who mourn shall be comforted (v. 4). The meek shall inherit the earth (v. 5). Those who hunger and thirst for righteousness shall be satisfied (v. 6). The merciful shall receive mercy (v. 7). The pure in heart shall see God (v. 8). The peacemakers shall be called sons of God (v. 9).

This seventh of the Beatitudes is the only place in the entire New Testament where the Greek word for "peacemakers" appears. There is considerable discussion of just what is meant by the term. At the very least it relates not just to passively keeping peace but also to the challenge of actively making peace with others embroiled in conflict, whether personally or helping to mediate between other parties.[10]

Please do not miss this. In this imposing and intimidating list of characteristics of the Christ-follower called "The Beatitudes," the question of how we deal with conflict is not optional. We cannot afford to be anything but peacemakers. When we are, when this characteristic sets us apart, when we're known for pursuing peace, when we help others achieve peace by our assistance, Jesus declares, "Blessed are you!" We enjoy a truly enviable status because he deems us worthy of a coveted title: "They shall be called sons of God."

What does he mean? A parallel usage of the same term helps answer the question:

> You have heard that it was said, "You shall love your neighbor and hate your enemy." But I say to you, Love your enemies and pray for those who persecute you, *so that you may be sons of your Father who is in heaven.* (Matt. 5:43–45, emphasis added)

What do peacemakers do in the face of conflict that involves persecution for some reason? Jesus commands, in contrast to conventional

151

wisdom, that they love their enemies and even pray for them. Why? That they may *be* sons of their Father who is in heaven.

To be called sons of God and to be sons of the Father are the same thing. Jesus is saying that to act like a peacemaker is to demonstrate the family character. It gives evidence that you belong to a Father called "the God of peace" (Heb. 13:20) who revealed himself in the Christ who came "reconciling the world to himself, not counting their trespasses against them, and entrusting to us the message of reconciliation" (2 Cor. 5:19). The payoff will come at the final judgment. Because of their faithful commitment to reconciling ways, God will reward peacemakers with that identity. He will bestow upon them the treasured label of "sons of God"—those worthy of enjoying his presence and privileges in heaven forever. Much rides on getting the peacemaking thing right! Matthew Henry drove it home this way:

> *They shall be called the children of God*; it will be an evidence to themselves that they are so; God will own them as such, and herein they will resemble him. He is the God of peace; the Son of God is the Prince of peace; the Spirit of adoption is a Spirit of peace. Since God has declared himself reconcilable to us all, he will not own those for his children who are implacable [impossible to appease] in their enmity to one another; for if the peacemakers are blessed, woe to the peace-breakers! . . . The children of this world love to fish in troubled waters, but the children of God are the peacemakers, *the quiet in the land*.[11]

Those who eagerly preserve the unity of the Spirit in the bond of peace (Eph. 4:3) enjoy priceless pleasures in their fellowships. They can sing the sweet song of unity in Psalm 133 and they will treasure forever the label "sons of God" in Matthew 5:9.

Dietrich Bonhoeffer, in his classic work on Christian community, *Life Together*, offered this counsel:

> The physical presence of other Christians is a source of incomparable joy and strength to the believer. . . . But if there is so much blessing and joy even in a single encounter of brother with brother, how inexhaustible are the riches that open up for those who by God's will are privileged to live in the daily fellowship of life with other Christians! It is true, of course, that what is an unspeakable gift of God for the lonely individual is easily disregarded and trodden under foot by those who have the gift

152

every day. It is easily forgotten that the fellowship of Christian brethren is a gift of grace, a gift of the Kingdom of God that any day may be taken from us, that the time that still separates us from utter loneliness may be brief indeed. Therefore, let him who until now has had the privilege of living in common Christian life with other Christians praise God's grace from the bottom of his heart. Let him thank God on his knees and declare: It is grace, nothing but grace, that we are allowed to live in community with Christian brethren.[12]

Amen! Let us do what Bonhoeffer exhorts. And let us continually do nothing less than our very best to preserve the extraordinary gift of unity for God's glory, our joy, and the church's mission.

Acknowledgments

In my journey as a peacemaker I owe a tremendous amount of gratitude to Peacemaker Ministries. Their successful intervention in our last church fight started a relationship that has profited me enormously as a pastor and now as an author writing on this subject. The resources, training, and personnel associated with the ministry have combined to help shape OGC into the peacemaking church it is today. Thanks be to God.

My journey as a writer started slow but would never have gotten off the ground without strategic help. Many thanks to John Gjertsen for nagging me into the blogosphere several years ago. Additional thanks to Mike Graham, my associate pastor, who put *Thinking Like Your Editor* into my hands. That resource charted my course for writing a proper book proposal for *The Peacemaking Church*. And Mike has remained my relentless cheerleader and advocate in this project. Also, I am fortunate for many reasons to have a band of brothers—I call them my armor bearers—who have kept on me to finish this project. I am grateful too for the support of my fellow elders and the people of OGC in encouraging me each step of the way, particularly through my personal suffering of the past three plus years.

As recounted in the book, my marital journey took a bizarre turn during my writing with the loss of Nancy, my wife of nearly forty-two years, to cancer. Nancy was a consummate peacemaker. No one helped me more over time in dealing with my anger. She backed me all the way in my writing and sacrificed hours of personal time with me in the process. Jan, my second gift bride from the Lord, has proven to be no less a champion of peace and oneness in our marriage. She too has given up time and cheered me on to the finish line. "He who finds a wife [in my case two] finds a good thing and obtains favor from the LORD" (Prov. 18:22). Jan graciously put her proofreading and editing eye on the manuscript at the end as well, for which I am also quite grateful.

Finally, many thanks to my friend and peacemaking mentor, Ken Sande, for encouraging me to write this book and for helping to open the publishing door. I am indebted to Jack Kuhatschek for enhancing my writing through his keen editorial skills. Bless you, Chad Allen and the entire Baker Books team, for your patience with numerous deadline extensions given my bereavement and medical leaves of absence.

Notes

Introduction

1. Charles Colson, *The Body: Being Light in Darkness* (Dallas: Word, 1992), 103.
2. Thom S. Rainer, "Twenty-Five Silly Things Church Members Fight Over," *Thom S. Rainer: Growing Healthy Churches, Together*, November 11, 2015, http://thomrainer .com/2015/11/twenty-five-silly-things-church-members-fight-over/.
3. Deidra Riggs, *One: Unity in a Divided World* (Grand Rapids: Baker, 2017), 25.
4. For more information regarding Peacemaker Ministries, see http://peacemaker .net/. For information on the new ministry that Ken Sande has launched to help people "get upstream of conflict," Relational Wisdom 360, see https://rw360.org.
5. For more information on various equipping options for conflict resolution, see "The Path of a Peacemaker" seminars available at http://pm.training/events/, and "Discovering Relational Wisdom 2.0" at https://Academy.rw360.org.
6. For a sampling of the available resources pertaining to resolving church conflict, see https://rw360.org/bookstore/.
7. For insight on preparing and making a robust confession of sin for resolving conflict and preserving peace, see "Seven A's of Confession," *Relational Wisdom 360*, accessed February 9, 2018, https://rw360.org/seven-as-of-confession/.
8. G. K. Chesterton, "A Thing Worth Doing," *The American Chesterton Society*, accessed February 15, 2018, https://www.chesterton.org/a-thing-worth-doing.

Chapter 1 Our Best and Nothing Less

1. D. Martyn Lloyd-Jones, *Christian Unity: An Exposition of Ephesians 4:1–10* (Grand Rapids: Baker, 1980), 41.
2. Markus Barth, as quoted in John R. W. Stott, *God's New Society: The Message of Ephesians* (Leicester, UK: Inter-Varsity Press, 1979), 153–54.
3. For insight on how forgiveness translates into concrete relational choices, see "Four Promises of Forgiveness," *Relational Wisdom 360*, accessed February 15, 2018, https://rw360.org/four-promises-of-forgiveness/.
4. For a description of options to pursue for help in peacemaking when individual efforts fail to succeed, see "Staying on Top of Conflict," *Peacemaker Ministries*, accessed February 15, 2018, http://peacemaker.net/project/slippery-slope/.

Chapter 2 Seeing Ourselves as Peacemakers in the Right Light

1. Stephanie Samuel, "Joni Eareckson Tada Encourages Optimism in Face of Trials," *The Christian Post*, May 6, 2011, http://christianpost.com/news/joni-eareckson-tada-encourages-optimism-in-face-of-trials-50126.html.

2. Leslie B. Flynn, *Great Church Fights* (Wheaton: Victor Books, 1976), 53.

3. Lawrence O. Richards and Clyde Hoeldtke, *A Theology of Church Leadership* (Grand Rapids: Zondervan, 1980), 48.

4. Eileen Rife, "A Prisoner of the Lord," *Bindings: Reflections on Faith, Life, and Good Books*, November 20, 2012, http://blogs.christianpost.com/bindings/a-prisoner-of-the-lord-13188.

5. Ken Sande, *The Peacemaker: A Biblical Guide to Resolving Personal Conflict*, third ed. (Grand Rapids: Baker, 2004), 259–61. Emphasis added.

6. Wayne Grudem, *Systematic Theology: An Introduction to Biblical Doctrine* (Leicester UK: Inter-Varsity Press, 1994), 693.

7. Timothy S. Lane and Paul David Tripp, *How People Change* (Greensboro, NC: New Growth Press, 2006), 79.

8. R. C. Sproul, *The Prayer of the Lord* (Lake Mary, FL: Reformation Trust, 2009), 82.

9. "St. Telemachus the Martyr," *News from the Underground: True Orthodox and Ecumenical News*, January 14, 2015, nftu.net/st-telemachus-martyr/.

Chapter 3 Shaping Our Approach as Peacemakers with the Right Touch

1. David A. Seamands, *Healing for Damaged Emotions* (Wheaton: Victor, 1981), 29–30.

2. Philip D. Yancey, *What's So Amazing about Grace?* (Grand Rapids: Zondervan, 1997), 229.

3. Thomas Watson, *The Godly Man's Picture* (Edinburgh: Banner of Truth Trust, 1992), 79.

4. Jonathan Edwards, *Charity and Its Fruits* (Edinburgh: Banner of Truth Trust, 1988), 131–32.

5. Paul David Tripp, *Dangerous Calling: Confronting the Unique Challenges of Pastoral Ministry* (Wheaton: Crossway, 2012), 21.

6. John Piper, "Maintain the Unity of the Spirit," *Desiring God*, May, 27, 1984, http://www.desiringgod.org/messages/maintain-the-unity-of-the-spirit.html.

7. Edwards, *Charity and Its Fruits*, 155.

8. Douglas Stone, Bruce Patton, and Sheila Heen, *Difficult Conversations: How to Discuss What Matters Most*, tenth anniversary ed. (New York: Penguin, 2010), 273.

9. Alexander Strauch, *A Christian Leader's Guide to Leading with Love* (Littleton, CO: Lewis & Roth Publishers, 2006), 45.

Chapter 4 Basing Our Thinking as Peacemakers on the Right Doctrine

1. R. C. Sproul, *Everyone's a Theologian: An Introduction to Systematic Theology* (Sanford, FL: Reformation Trust, 2014), 12.

2. Ross Douthat, *Bad Religion: How We Became a Nation of Heretics* (New York: Free Press, 2012), 3–4.

3. We subscribe to the 1689 London Baptist Confession of Faith. For a modern-day English version of the document, visit http://soulreach.org/bcf.

4. Tara Klena Barthel and Judy Dabler, *Peacemaking Women: Biblical Hope for Resolving Conflict* (Grand Rapids: Baker, 2005), 21.

5. A. W. Tozer, *The Knowledge of the Holy* (New York: HarperCollins, 1961), 1.

6. For an excellent treatment of how God can be three persons yet one God, see Grudem, "God in Three Persons: The Trinity," *Systematic Theology*, 226–59.

7. Lloyd-Jones, *Christian Unity*, 49.

8. Edmund P. Clowney, *The Church: Contours of Christian Theology* (Downers Grove, IL: InterVarsity Press, 1995), 79.

9. Barthel and Dabler, *Peacemaking Women*, 222–23.

10. *The Bylaws of Orlando Grace Church* (revised March 22, 2015).

11. Mark Dever and Paul Alexander, *The Deliberate Church: Building Your Ministry on the Gospel* (Wheaton: Crossway, 2005), 28. For more information on the ministry of 9Marks, see http://9marks.org.

12. Thomas Goodwin, as quoted in John Piper, *Think: The Life of the Mind and the Love of God* (Wheaton: Crossway, 2010), 90.

13. Thomas Watson, as quoted in Charles H. Spurgeon, *The Treasury of David* (Peabody, MA: Hendrickson, 1988), 171.

14. Riggs, *One*, 25.

Chapter 5 Murdering

1. Alfred Poirier, *The Peacemaking Pastor: A Biblical Guide to Resolving Church Conflict* (Grand Rapids: Baker, 2006), 277.

2. Alexander Strauch, *If You Bite & Devour One Another: Biblical Principles for Handling Conflict* (Littleton, CO: Lewis and Roth, 2011), 51.

3. Sinclair Ferguson, *The Sermon on the Mount: Kingdom Life in a Fallen World* (Edinburgh: Banner of Truth Trust, 1987), 67–68.

4. Christopher Ash, *Listen Up! A Practical Guide to Listening to Sermons* (Surrey, UK: The Good Book Company, 2009), 8.

5. I am indebted to Paul Tripp for this hitting-all-too-close-to-home metaphor for my self-defense mechanisms in *Dangerous Calling*, 17.

6. For a classic though demanding treatment on the subject of putting sin to death, see John Owen, *The Mortification of Sin* (Edinburgh: Banner of Truth Trust, 2004).

7. Lane and Tripp, *How People Change*, 16.

8. Les Carter and Frank Minirth, *The Anger Workbook* (Nashville: Thomas Nelson, 1993), 4.

9. Robert D. Jones, *Uprooting Anger: Biblical Help for a Common Problem* (Phillipsburg, NJ: P&R, 2005), 21.

10. Carter and Minirth, *Anger Workbook*, 236.

11. For an exhaustive list of helpful "X-Ray Questions" for examining potential heart idols behind any number of sinful behavior patterns, see Lane and Tripp, *How People Change*, 163–65.

12. Lane and Tripp, *How People Change*, 190.

13. Jones, *Uprooting Anger*, 160.

14. Flynn, *Great Church Fights*, 84.

15. Charles Spurgeon, *Sermon on the Mount* (Grand Rapids: Baker, 1979), 27.
16. Sande, *Peacemaker*, 90.
17. Jones, *Uprooting Anger*, 109.
18. Martin Luther, *A Simple Way to Pray*, trans. Matthew C. Harrison (St. Louis: Concordia, 2012), 23–24.

Chapter 6 Litigating

1. Justice Antonin Scalia, "Teaching About the Law," *Quarterly* 7, no. 4 (Fall 1987): 8–9.
2. Ray Stedman, "The Wrong Way to Right Wrongs," *Authentic Christianity*, August 27, 1978, https://www.raystedman.org/new-testament/1-corinthians/the-wrong-way-to-right-wrongs.
3. J. Stanley Glen, *Pastoral Problems in First Corinthians* (London: Epworth, 1965), 79.
4. Marion L. Soards, *1 Corinthians* (Grand Rapids: Baker, 1999), 123.
5. Ben Witherington III, *Conflict and Community in Corinth* (Grand Rapids: Eerdmans, 1995), 164.
6. Sande, *Peacemaker*, 279–82.
7. William Barclay, *The Letters to the Corinthians* (Philadelphia: Westminster Press, 1975), 49.
8. Barclay, *Letters to the Corinthians*, 49–50.
9. Charles Hodge, *An Exposition of the First Epistle to the Corinthians* (Grand Rapids: Eerdmans, 1969), 93.
10. Poirier, *Peacemaking Pastor*, 215–16.
11. Witherington, *Conflict and Community in Corinth*, 165.
12. N. T. Wright, *Surprised by Hope: Rethinking Heaven, the Resurrection, and the Mission of the Church* (New York: HarperOne, 2008), 144.
13. Preben Vang, *1 Corinthians* (Grand Rapids: Baker, 2014), 72.
14. The Greek term is *strong*. It is translated "despised" in 1 Cor. 1:28, characterizing the Corinthians in their unsaved state.
15. Bruce W. Winter, *After Paul Left Corinth* (Grand Rapids: Eerdmans, 2001), 70.
16. Paige Patterson, *The Troubled, Triumphant Church: An Exposition of First Corinthians* (Nashville: Thomas Nelson, 1983), 100.
17. Sande, *Peacemaker*, 280.
18. Patterson, *Troubled, Triumphant Church*, 98.
19. Alan F. Johnson, *1 Corinthians: The IVP New Testament Commentary Series* (Downers Grove, IL: InterVarsity Press, 2004), 95.
20. Craig L. Blomberg, *1 Corinthians* (Grand Rapids: Zondervan, 1994), 118.
21. H. A. Ironside, "Ironside's Notes on Selected Books: 1 Corinthians 6," *Study Light*, accessed February 13, 2018, https://www.studylight.org/commentaries/isn/1-corinthians-6.html.
22. For a thorough treatment of these subjects see Jonathan Leeman and Mark Dever, *The Church and the Surprising Offense of God's Love: Reintroducing the Doctrines of Church Membership and Discipline* (Wheaton: Crossway, 2010).
23. Peacemaker Ministries, "Resolving Everyday Conflict Kit," accessed February 13, 2018, http://peacemaker.net/resolving-everyday-conflict-new.

24. Richard L. Pratt and Max E. Anders, *I & II Corinthians* (Nashville: Broadman & Holman, 2000), 87.

25. Blomberg, *1 Corinthians*, 122. See esp. H. Wayne House, "Reconciling Disputes Among Christians," in *Christian Ministries and the Law*, ed. H. Wayne House (Grand Rapids: Baker, 1992), 79–88, for a description of the Christian conciliation process, and "Appendix D," 219–20, for a sampling of some of the Christian conciliation ministries of North America.

26. John Calvin, "Institutes of the Christian Religion: Chapter 20, Of Civil Government," *Christian Classics Ethereal Library*, accessed February 13, 2018, https://www.ccel.org/ccel/calvin/institutes.vi.xxi.html.

Chapter 7 Judging

1. Strauch, *If You Bite & Devour One Another*, 83–84.

2. Source unknown.

3. Christina Cleveland, *Disunity in Christ: Uncovering the Hidden Forces That Keep Us Apart* (Downers Grove, IL: InterVarsity Press, 2013), 31.

4. James Boice, *The New Humanity (Romans 12–16)*, vol. 4, *Romans* (Grand Rapids: Baker, 1995), 1728.

5. Matthew Henry, *Acts to Revelation*, vol. 6, *Commentary on the Whole Bible* (McLean, VA: Macdonald, 1985), 485.

6. John Piper, "We Will All Stand Before the Judgment of God," *Desiring God*, October 30, 2005, http://www.desiringgod.org/messages/we-will-all-stand-before-the-judgment-of-god.

7. Warren Wiersbe, *Be Right* (Wheaton: Victor, 1977), 162.

8. For helpful resources on the gospel, see D. A. Carson and Tim Keller, eds., *The Gospel as Center: Renewing Our Faith and Reforming Our Ministry Practices* (Wheaton: Crossway, 2012); Matt Chandler, *The Explicit Gospel* (Wheaton: Crossway, 2012); Greg Gilbert, *What Is the Gospel?* (Wheaton: Crossway, 2010); J. D. Greear, *Gospel: Recovering the Power That Made Christianity Revolutionary* (Nashville: Broadman & Holman, 2011).

9. For passages related to the future judgment of the believer, see Matt. 12.36; 25:31–46; Luke 19:17, 19; Acts 17:30–31; Rom. 2:5–11; 14:10, 12; 1 Cor. 3:10–15; 4:5; 2 Cor. 5:10; Rev. 20:11–15.

10. Francis Schaeffer, *The Mark of a Christian* (Downers Grove, IL: InterVarsity Press, 1970), 15.

11. Max Lucado, *In the Grip of Grace* (Dallas: Word Publishing, 1996), 160–63.

Chapter 8 Intercepting Relational Disasters before They Ever Occur

1. Harriet Beecher Stowe, *The Writings of Harriet Beecher Stowe: With Biographical Introductions, Portraits and Other Illustrations* (Boston: Houghton Mifflin, 1896), 414.

2. As quoted in *Proceedings*, vol. 31, American Gas Association (1949): 175.

3. Source unknown.

4. "Magnanimous," *English Oxford Living Dictionaries*, accessed February 14, 2018, https://en.oxforddictionaries.com/definition/magnanimous.

5. For an excellent treatment of the means of grace crucial to an altar-building lifestyle for the believer, see Grudem, "Means of Grace within the Church," *Systematic Theology*, 950–65.

6. Matthew Henry, *Genesis to Deuteronomy*, vol. 1 of *Commentary on the Whole Bible* (McLean, VA: Macdonald, 1985), 87.

7. Bruce K. Waltke, *The Book of Proverbs: Chapters 15–31* (Grand Rapids: Eerdmans, 2005), 129.

8. Poirier, *Peacemaking Pastor*, 105.

9. Tim Lane and Paul Tripp, *Relationships: A Mess Worth Making* (Greensboro, NC: New Growth Press, 2006), 44.

10. John Calvin, *Genesis*, vol. 1 of *Calvin's Commentaries* (Grand Rapids: Baker, 1999), 373.

11. Ligonier Ministries, "Abram Settled," *Tabletalk*, March 5, 2018, https://www.ligonier.org/learn/devotionals/abram-settled.

12. William Vanderbloemen and Warren Bird, *Next: Pastoral Succession That Works* (Grand Rapids: Baker, 2014), 121.

Chapter 9 Honoring Spiritual Leaders for Their Exceptional Work

1. Tara Klena Barthel and David V. Edling, *Redeeming Church Conflicts: Turning Crisis into Compassion and Care* (Grand Rapids: Baker, 2012), 152.

2. For a compendium of these sermons, see Ian Hamish Murray, *Sermons of the Great Ejection* (Edinburgh; Carlisle, PA: Banner of Truth Trust, 2012).

3. Thomas Brooks, "The Legacies of Thomas Brooks," *Fire and Ice: Puritan and Reformed Writings*, January 25, 1999, http://www.puritansermons.com/sermons/brooks1.htm.

4. Leon Morris, *The Epistles of Paul to the Thessalonians* (Grand Rapids: Eerdmans, 1958), 99.

5. Barthel and Edling, *Redeeming Church Conflicts*, 152.

6. For a helpful treatment of the importance of church membership, see Jonathan Leeman, *Church Membership: How the World Knows Who Represents Jesus* (Wheaton: Crossway, 2012).

7. Poirier, *Peacemaking Pastor*, 283.

8. David Mathis, "Embrace the Blessing of Rebuke," *Desiring God*, August 27, 2014, http://www.desiringgod.org/articles/embrace-the-blessing-of-rebuke.

9. Barthel and Edling, *Redeeming Church Conflicts*, 153–54.

Epilogue

1. Paul Rees, as quoted in Strauch, *If You Bite & Devour One Another*, 116.

2. Tierney Sneed, "Study: Pop Music's Themes Are a Sign of the Times," *US News and World Report*, March 19, 2014, https://www.usnews.com/news/articles/2014/03/19/study-culls-thematic-trends-of-last-50-years-of-pop-hits-to-aid-advertisers?int=news-rec.

3. Charles Spurgeon, *Treasury of David*, vol. 3 (Peabody, MA: Hendrickson, 1988), 167.

4. W. Ewing, "Hermon," *International Standard Bible Encyclopedia*, 1915, http://www.bible-history.com/isbe/H/HERMON/.

5. Strauch, *If You Bite & Devour One Another*, 109.

6. See "Psalm 133," *Seedbed*, accessed February 14, 2018, http://psalms.seedbed.com/psalm-133/, for one possible rendition of Psalm 133.

7. For a notable exception written by some of the finest artists of the day, see "Oh How Good It Is," *Getty Music*, accessed February 14, 2018, http://www.gettymusic.com/oh-how-good-it-is/.

8. Ligon Duncan, "The Joy of Unity," LigonDuncan.com, June 12, 2012, http://ligonduncan.com/the-joy-of-unity-534/.

9. Eugene Peterson, *A Long Obedience in the Same Direction: Discipleship in an Instant Society* (Downers Grove, IL: InterVarsity Press,1980), 173.

10. Strauch, *If You Bite & Devour One Another*, 108.

11. Matthew Henry, *Commentary on the Whole Bible*, vol. 5 (McLean, VA: Macdonald Publishing, 1985), 52.

12. Dietrich Bonhoeffer, *Life Together: The Classic Exploration of Christian Community* (New York: Harper and Row, 1954), 19–20.

Subject Index

Scripture Index

Connect with Curt

CurtHeffelfinger.com

GO ONLINE FOR

- Blog updates
- Contacting Curt
- More book info

 @RevHeff

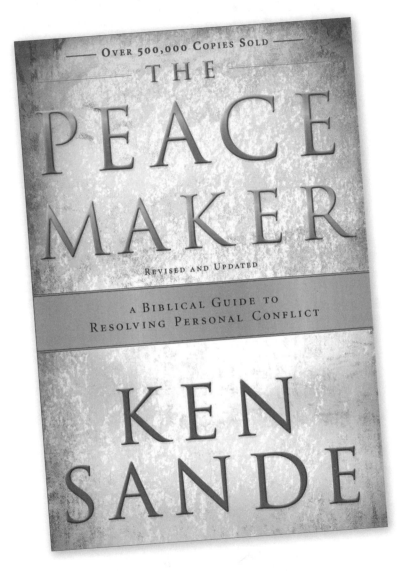

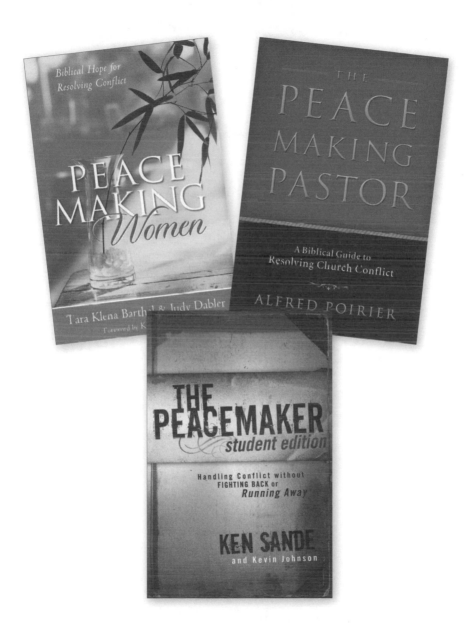